JOSEPH WHITE MUSSER

Introductions to Mormon Thought

Edited by Matthew Bowman and Joseph Spencer
*For a list of books in the series, please see our website
at* www.press.uillinois.edu.

JOSEPH WHITE MUSSER

A Mormon Fundamentalist

CRISTINA M. ROSETTI

UNIVERSITY OF
ILLINOIS PRESS
Urbana, Chicago, and Springfield

Library of Congress Cataloging-in-Publication Data
Names: Rosetti, Cristina, author.
Title: Joseph White Musser : a Mormon fundamentalist /
    Cristina M. Rosetti.
Other titles: Introductions to Mormon thought.
Description: Urbana : University of Illinois Press, [2023] |
    Series: Introductions to Mormon thought | Includes
    bibliographical references and index.
Identifiers: LCCN 2023024550 (print) | LCCN 2023024551 (ebook) |
    ISBN 9780252045639 (cloth) | ISBN 9780252087752 (paperback)
    | ISBN 9780252055300 (ebook)
Subjects: LCSH: Musser, Joseph W. | Mormons—Biography. |
    Ex-church members—Church of Jesus Christ of Latter-day
    Saints—Biography. | Mormon fundamentalism—History—
    20th century. | LCGFT: Biographies.
Classification: LCC BX8695.M87 R67 2023 (print) |
    LCC BX8695.M87 (ebook) | DDC 289.3092—dc23/eng/20230712
LC record available at https://lccn.loc.gov/2023024550
LC ebook record available at https://lccn.loc.gov/2023024551

For the Mormons who call Joseph W. Musser a prophet.

A Tribute to a Friend: Joseph White Musser

—Deacon Jarbee, December 10, 1944

A tribute we pay to a good man and true:
He's tolerant, forgiving: he's loyal, true blue;
He's faithful courageous, he's honest and fine;
He stands by precepts of things that are divine.
Rebuker of evil, a leader of men—
The man we refer to? It is J.W.M.

Many years have passed by, but time has been kind.
His eyes clear and sparkling; he has a keen mind.
His hair white as snow, and a moustache the same.
All kinds of weather whether sunshine or rain
Answers calls for his blessing, at two or ten,
He comforts and he helps all, does J.W.M.

His step is ecstatic, his shoulders are square,
His conscience is clear and his countenance fair.
Fearing no earthly man, nor what man can do;
Things we suffer for, are best for me and you;
Never give up Gospel truths: creeds he'll defend.
These are things that he fights for, does J.W.M.

We hope he stays with us for a long time to come,
But when he goes on to the "Glory of the Sun,"
There'll be Joseph and Hyrum, Brigham and John
To welcome him home to the place he has won.
The Lord will receive him and say to him then,
"Well done, good and faithful brother, J.W.M."

They'll all crowd around him and close to the throne.
The torch he'd held high when to him it was thrown.
He'd never reviled those who sought his downfall,
But he kept his eyes straight and ignored one and all.
Who tried to persuade him to desert what to them
Was the wrong path to take: That's J.W.M.

He's loved by the faithful, despised by the false;
He is human, so he has his virtues and faults.
When his life's page is written we're sure you'll find
His fault will be minute, his virtues sublime.
For his faith in the Priesthood we'll all say "Amen."
A True Gospel champion is J.W.M.

Contents

Foreword to the Introductions to Mormon Thought Series

Our purpose in this series is to provide readers with accessible and short introductions to important figures in the intellectual life of the religious movement that traces its origins to the prophetic career of Joseph Smith Jr. With an eye to the many branches of that movement (rather than solely to its largest branch, the Church of Jesus Christ of Latter-day Saints), the series gathers studies of what scholars have long called *Mormon* thought. We define "thought" and "intellectual life," however, quite as broadly as we define "Mormonism." We understand these terms to be inclusive, not simply of formal theological or scholarly work, but also of artistic production, devotional writing, institutional influence, political activism, and other non-scholarly pursuits. In short, volumes in the series assess the contributions of men and women who have shaped how those called Mormons in various traditions think about what "Mormonism" is.

We hope that this series marks something of a coming of age of scholarship on this religious tradition. For many years, Mormon studies have focused primarily on historical questions largely of internal interest to the (specifically) Latter-day Saint community. Such historical work has also mainly addressed the nineteenth century. Scholars have accordingly established the key sources for the study of Mormon history and culture, and they have established a broad consensus on many issues surrounding the origins and character of the religious movement. Recent work, however, has pushed academics into the work of comparison, asking larger questions in two key ways. First, recent scholars have approached these topics from a greater variety of disciplines. There has emerged in Mormon studies, in other words, increasing visibility for the disciplines of philosophy, sociology, literary criticism, and media studies, among others. Second, scholars working this field have also begun to consider new topics of study—in particular, gender and sexuality, the status of international Mormonism, and the experience of minority groups within the tradition. We believe the field has thus reached the point where the sort of syntheses these books offer is both possible and needed.

Cristina Rosetti's study of Joseph Musser fulfills many aims of the series, and we are excited to include it in *Introductions to Mormon Thought*. Musser abandoned the Church of Jesus Christ of Latter-day Saints to pursue his own form of Mormonism, one he believed to more fully embody what he understood as the religion's imperatives. His life and thought thus encourage us to think about borders and boundaries in religion, as well as the messy intersections between various manifestations of the Latter-day Saint movement. Especially encouraging is the way that Rosetti uses Musser to think more broadly about "fundamentalism," a concept emerging from US Protestantism that, for scholars and journalists and even religious people generally, has become an increasingly useful category for analysis and self-expression. Mormon fundamentalism is a long-understudied phenomenon, and Rosetti's work is a much-needed contribution to its analysis. We hope this book will help readers better understand the Mormon movement in particular and the modern phenomenon of religious fundamentalism more broadly.

Matthew Bowman
Joseph Spencer

Acknowledgments

Saint Joseph White Musser's story, and the story of Mormon fundamentalism, is housed in archives, homes, and oral traditions across the Intermountain West. Many people sought to compile and tell his story in the last few decades, breaking open these records and uncovering the history of Mormonism's alternate twentieth-century trajectory. Several acknowledgments are necessary for the efforts of these people and those who supported this project.

First and foremost, I am grateful to the many families who welcomed me into their homes and shared their ardent faith in the doctrine Musser espoused and the priesthood he possessed. If Musser's thought continues into the Millennium, it will be because of the people who maintain their faith despite the continued criminalization of their religion. This book is dedicated to them.

Brian Hales received unprecedented access to Musser's journals and letters before others had the same access to the archival record. His willingness to make the primary sources widely available is too often underrecognized in Mormon studies. The transcriptions from these sources are a vital resource in fundamentalist history and his research remains among the most widely read on the subject. Craig Foster, Marianne Watson, Newell G. Bringhurst, D. Michael Quinn, Ken Driggs, and Martha Sonntag Bradley similarly produced foundational work on Musser and the polygamous Mormons of Short Creek. They shaped the field and broadened Mormon studies to include underrepresented voices. Their work inspired my interest in Mormon fundamentalism and informed how I tell history.

This project would not have been possible without the immense support of Bryan Buchanan, who waded through documents, transcribed primary sources, and offered a friendly ear that was always excited about historical findings. For his transcription of Musser's later journals, the "Book of Remembrance" and Woolley's "School of the Prophets," I am particularly thankful. I am grateful to Matthew Bowman and Joseph Spencer, who saw Musser's life as significant in the broader history of Mormonism and welcomed his inclusion in this series. Daisy Vargas, Lindsay Hansen Park, Jacob Newman, and Scott Barrett heard ideas and read portions of drafts. The support of friends and colleagues proved to be among the most significant contributors to this project's completion. In the final months before publication, Joseph Stuart indexed this book. I am immensely thankful for his careful eye and encouragement throughout the process.

My family listened to me talk about the life of a widely unknown character in Mormon history for more than three years with patience and grace. They deserve eternal thanks. Most significantly, Giuseppe Gagliano read more issues of *Truth* magazine than anyone else I know and loved me through the most challenging months of writing and editing. His love is the greatest gift.

JOSEPH WHITE MUSSER

CHAPTER ONE

Saint Joseph White Musser

Prologue

On July 17, 1902, John M. Murdock, a patriarch of the Church of Jesus Christ of Latter-day Saints, laid his hands on Saint Joseph White Musser's head and offered a blessing.[1] At the time of the blessing, Musser was thirty years old and had long been engaged in Church service as a missionary in the southern states, had served as a member of the 105th First Quorum of the Seventy, and had received his second anointing. In his role as patriarch, Murdock spoke on behalf of God and proclaimed, "A great and mighty work lies before you; therefore, dear brother, prepare thine heart to receive the revelations of the Lord that will come unto you."[2] Within two decades of the blessing, the Church excommunicated Musser for continuing the practice of plural marriage after the official Church statements in 1890 and 1904 that commanded an end to the practice. Like many others during that fraught time, Musser's excommunication was not the end of his involvement in Mormonism but the beginning of his participation in a religious movement that sought to preserve a vision of Joseph Smith's religious innovation lost in the twentieth century.

Musser's life is part of one of the most difficult periods in Mormon history, the long end to polygamy and the ambiguous position in which it placed many Latter-day Saints. While faithful to the religious principles he learned as a child, he found himself at odds with his religious institution, which he believed too willingly caved to social and political pressure. The tension between his ardent faith and his loss of membership in his religious community became the catalyst for much of Musser's theological innovation about the nature of religious authority and temporal institutions. His life is indicative of how difficult it was for the Church to disentangle itself from dissident Mormons who continued the practice of polygamy into the twentieth century. At the same time, the documents Musser produced to make sense of his experience garnered converts who were similarly disenfranchised by the Church of Jesus Christ of Latter-day Saints.

Mormon polygamists were not alone in their search for an authentic religion that preserved the fundamentals. The twentieth century was a difficult time for all people who saw the rise of modernity as a challenge to their faith and a cause for concern. In the wake of new scientific ideas, innovative ways of interpreting biblical text, and the emergence of the social gospel, the Christian fundamentalist movement developed as a reactionary response.[3] Mormon fundamentalism emerged in the context of this broader fundamentalist movement. They sought preservation in light of what they perceived as an inappropriate response to modernity from their LDS counterparts. Fundamentalist Mormonism, as with fundamentalism broadly, frequently asserts itself as the more original version of the religion. In actuality, fundamentalism is inextricably modern.

It cannot be understated that Mormon fundamentalism is a modern religion. The first iterations of the movement emerged in 1922 at Nathaniel Baldwin's home, the inventor of headphones and founder of the Baldwin Radio Company. The men and women present at the meeting were modern people, indistinguishable from anyone else in twentieth-century Utah. While the LDS Church succumbed to the "invisible consensus of American Protestantism," Mormon fundamentalists position themselves as the most authentic expression of Mormonism and one that resembles the nineteenth-century faith that met on the banks of the Missouri River.[4] While Mormon fundamentalism is notably different in its approach to modern LDS Mormonism, its adherents are, nevertheless, fully modern people participating in a fully modern faith.

Many people familiar with the origins of Mormon fundamentalism acknowledge the significance of Lorin C. Woolley, the man who first articulated an alternate priesthood history meant to retain the practice of plural marriage. But Woolley did not keep a diary or transcribe his sermons. What we know about Woolley's early fundamentalist history and doctrinal formation came through the writings of Musser. As shown in Musser's intellectual contributions, the earliest iteration of Mormon fundamentalism grew from a disparate collection of outcast men and women into a distinct movement that captured the attention of the institutional LDS Church and the nation. His work became a useful tool for the LDS Church, as he served as the foil by which the Church of Jesus Christ of Latter-day Saints became increasingly accepted within the American religious landscape. It is my belief that Musser would have wanted to be remembered for embodying the ardent resolve to retain the fundamentals of Mormonism, even those that seemed strange or antiquated to outsiders, as well as for being a thorn in the side of the LDS Church. It was his success as both that made Musser one of the most significant contributors to Mormon intellectual thought in the twentieth century.

Early Life and Church Service (1872–1909)

Saint Joseph White Musser was born to Amos Milton Musser and his first plural wife, Mary White Musser, on March 8, 1872. In addition to his biological mother, Musser noted his father's marriages to Ann Leaver, Belinda Marden Pratt, and Anna Seegmiller. Together, Musser's father had thirty-five children, ten from Mary White. Musser reflected on his life as one "nurtured in the Patriarchal Law," a principle he unquestionably believed.[6] Polygamy was inherently part of what it meant to be Mormon. From an early age, Musser saw his father perform faithful service to the Church in a variety of callings. His father worked in the Church Historian's Office, served as clerk of the tithing office, acted as a traveling bishop, and served a mission in the eastern United States. For his faithful involvement in plural marriage, a principle he taught his children was a necessary and unchangeable tenet of the faith, Amos Milton Musser ultimately served time in the Utah territorial prison from May 13, 1885, to October 12, 1885, and paid a $300 fine for the criminal practice. Musser eventually followed in his father's footsteps and, after the 1944 government raid on the polygamous Mormons in Salt Lake City and southern Utah, served the same sentence beginning on March 7, 1944, for the same crime.

Church participation was a hallmark of Musser's early life. At the age of twelve, his father ordained him to the Aaronic priesthood, and he assumed the role of deacon. He was subsequently ordained a teacher and priest, the expected religious trajectory of young men in the Church. While he recalled most of his education in the "school of hard knocks," Musser briefly attended Latter-day Saints' University, now Ensign College, as one of the first students in the program.[7] His lack of formal education did not prevent him from continued employment. From his first job as a cow herder at the age of ten, working in the mining, electrical, and agricultural industries was a constant part of his life As an adult, "routine work" became his most common diary entry, a sentence that encapsulated Musser's work ethic and striving to provide for a growing family. Despite these efforts, financial insecurity occupied much of his daily recollection and memories. His participation in plural marriage only exacerbated his financial precarity and shaped his steadfast belief in Mormon communitarianism.

Although Musser fondly remembered his polygamous upbringing, his family system was a point of contention that positioned his Church at odds with the United States government. The 1882 Edmunds Act and 1887 Edmunds-Tucket Act disincorporated the Church and put Church asserts at risk of seizure. With the Church and its temples hanging in the balance, President Wilford Woodruff signed Official Declaration 1, colloquially known as the First Manifesto or the Woodruff Manifesto. The 1890 document declared, "We are not teaching polygamy or plural marriage, nor permitting any person to enter into its practice, and I deny that either forty or any other number of plural marriages have during that period been solemnized in our Temples or in any other place in the Territory."[8] In retrospect, the manifesto began the long process of aligning the institution with its Protestant counterparts. While the language of the document was stern, convincing the nation of the Church's resolve and its ability to fully end plural marriage proved more complicated.

Only two years after the Woodruff Manifesto, in 1892, Musser married his first wife, Rose Selms Borquist, in the Logan, Utah, Temple. Until they settled in Forest Dale, Utah, in 1894, the young couple lived with Musser's parents in a rented room. In Forest Dale, presently a historic district in Salt Lake City, Musser was set apart for his mission to the southern states by Brigham Young Jr., Heber J. Grant, John W. Taylor, and Abraham H. Cannon. Musser's mission was formative, solidifying his convictions in the faith through multiple instances of healing and spiritual growth. At the same time, he recounted encountering mockery from outsiders who ridiculed the Mormon marriage system, something Musser ardently believed. He recalled, "Mormon polygamy is criticized by the most unmoral [sic] men, and who usually can be hushed up in a moment by bold reference to the sins they [are] darkly blasting virtue with."[9] While Musser does not reflect on the criticism from those he sought to convert on his mission, the need to defend the practice from a young age shaped his conviction of the necessity of the controversial marital system.

Central to his mission experience was President J. Golden Kimball, a leader with whom Musser remained in contact for the duration of Kimball's life. In entries to his mission diary, Musser recalled Kimball prophesying that the young missionaries in the southern states would "preside over our brethren in Zion."[10] "His eyes watered up as he prophesied in the name of the Lord that I will sometime become a great [m]an in the eyes of God unless I rebel and fight the Lord," recalling a blessing he received from Kimball.[11] Musser's blessings from leaders throughout his life promised nothing short of greatness, something he recalled later in life when many of the same leaders who blessed him and set him apart for service became his harshest critics.

Two years after he returned from his mission, on November 30, 1899, President Lorenzo Snow invited Musser and Rose to receive their second anointing in the Logan Temple. For many Latter-day Saints, a second anointing is a significant life event that marks both devotion to the Gospel and faithfulness to the institutional Church. Theologically, the anointing raises the participants to the status of "king and priest" or "queen and priestess" and ensures the couple's exaltation to the highest degree of the Celestial Kingdom. For the couple involved, the ritual confers the highest authority available in the Church, sometimes elevating the participants above their local leadership. Because of the sacredness of the ordinance that established the anointing, Musser does not offer much detail or information about the experience. In his diary, he simply noted that "myself and wife were permitted to receive glorious blessings in the Temple; We took advantage of this day for same."[12] In the margins of the entry, Musser circled the words "Temple Blessings."[13] The highest ordinance of the Church was conferred upon the young couple when they were just twenty-seven years old.

The second anointing was a pivotal moment in the life of Musser's young Mormon family. An event that occurred several days after, however, became the catalyst for the remainder of their Church experience and put their institutional faithfulness to the test. In his autobiographical sketch, Musser recalled a day in December 1899 when "a messenger came to me from President Snow, stating I had been selected to enter plural marriage and to help keep the principle alive. Apprising my wife of the situation we both entered into prayer for guidance."[14] Acknowledging the 1890 Manifesto, he explained his complicated position: "God's Prophet told me to accept the law and keep it alive. His subordinates said if I did so, they would cut me off the Church."[15]

Although there is no contemporary evidence aside from Musser's recollections that affirm Snow's involvement in Musser's postmanifesto polygamous marriages, support existed within the Church from members of the Quorum of the Twelve Apostles and his local congregation. This included the postmanifesto marriages authorized by Joseph F. Smith. To attest the matter further, Musser frequently recorded diary entries from Church meetings in which local leaders preached the necessity of plural marriage from the pulpit. Musser's stake president William H. Smart supported Musser's polygamous sealing to Mary C. Hill and was himself polygamously sealed by Elder Matthias F. Cowley.[16] Despite the numerous polygamous unions solemnized around him, perpetuating plural marriage still presented a risk. The call to perpetuate polygamy offered two options: Musser could obey the man he deemed a Prophet and continue the practice of polygamy at the possible expense of his Church membership or continue his monogamous marriage with Rose and remain a faithful member of the Church. Musser chose the former.

Musser's diaries do not specify Rose's immediate reaction to the supposed messenger. But, soon after, in 1901, Rose expressed her support for plural marriage and willingness to live the principle. "At night had a splendid talk with Rose on the subject of Plural Marriage. She is fully converted to the principle, and says she believes we will have to practice it before long. She is trying to prepare herself for the principle," Musser recalled in his diary.[17] In November that year, Rose approached Musser ready to live the principle and suggested a woman she felt was a good fit for their family. Of their conversation, Musser recorded that, "For this testimony given to my wife, I am truly grateful to the Lord, and it shall be my desire through life, whether living in that principle or not, to live worthy of receiving to myself wives and children according to the will of God."[18]

Shortly after this exchange with his wife, Musser began a courtship with Mary Caroline Hill, a woman he met through a ministering relationship with her ill brother. At the time of the courtship, Musser was president of the 105th Quorum of the Seventy and a member of his stake High Council.[19] Mary's father, William Hood Hill, needed persuading about his daughter's decision to marry Musser in a postmanifesto sealing. Hill served in his bishopric when Musser met his daughter. Before his tenure in local leadership, Hill spent time in prison alongside Musser's father for polygamy. For this reason, and because of the Church "handling people for proposing it," Hill expressed concern about his daughter's well-being and her standing in the Church.[20] He quickly acceded, however, after learning Musser received a blessing from the Church to continue the practice of polygamy. Elders John Henry Smith and Matthias F. Cowley confirmed the blessing to Hill, who allowed the marriage.

Two months after Mary's father gave his approval, on March 13, 1902, Musser was sealed to her under the sealing authority of Matthias Cowley in Salt Lake City.[21] Aside from one confidential meeting on January 14, 1902, with Elder Matthias Cowley, nothing was recorded about the courtship. The sealing records of the men who solemnized such unions became a testament that managing the family structure was a difficult institutional task, a task that was only compounded by the theological significance of plural marriage before 1890. Only two years after Musser's second marriage, the LDS Church again sought to reassure the nation that the Woodruff Manifesto ended plural marriage. The Second Manifesto, spoken from the pulpit by Joseph F. Smith in 1904, would be the Church's second attempt to end the practice that made the LDS Church notorious in the eyes of its neighbors.

Scant record keeping was not uncommon for plural relationships in this period, when the Church increasingly distanced itself from polygamous unions. On the day of the sealing, Musser wrote, "Attended wedding of my friend—Mr. Grant, who was joined in holy union to Mrs. Rae." The following July, "Mrs. Rae" appeared for the second and last time in journals, with no connection to Mary C. Hill. Musser never mentioned his own sealing to Mary. References to Mary as one of his wives appear suddenly and without context. The possibility of "Mr. Grant" and "Mrs. Rae" acting as pseudonyms for his sealing is speculative. The date corresponds with Cowley's sealing record, however, and with Musser's autobiographic timeline.

Shortly after his sealing to Hill, Musser visited Homer Duncan, a man whose unmarried daughter died at the age of thirty. During their meeting, Duncan inquired about a potential sealing between his deceased daughter and Musser. (In LDS cosmology, proxy ordinances for the dead provide the deceased an avenue for salvation and exaltation, specifically those unable to participate during their lives.) Recalling the encounter, Musser explained,

"May was a sweet girl and I feel very grateful for the privilege of having her sealed to me, but of course, I accept the trust on condition it is agreeable to her, otherwise, I expect her desires to prevail in eternity."[22] Musser did not discuss an actual sealing to May, and a sealing record is not extant. But these sealings remain a central feature of Mormon marital cosmology, calling into question the extent to which polygamy remained part of Mormon temple worship within the institutional LDS Church. While May was not physically present in the proposed sealing, the ritual would have been a valid plural sealing in the eyes of the Church and the involved families, making May Duncan a posthumous wife of Joseph W. Musser.

As the husband of multiple wives, Musser continued his Church service and advanced within the hierarchy. During this time, his public support for plural marriage never wavered. He publicly proclaimed the truthfulness of the marital practice and its central place in Mormon cosmology from the pulpit at Church meetings. Representative of such testimonies was a meeting held in May 1902:

> Attended 70 meeting. Prest. Smart and Bro Jensen were visitors. In bearing my testimony, I spoke of plural marriage as being an essential principle of the Gospel and the brethren should not only believe in it, but pray for its return and prepare themselves to live it. Bro Jensen + Tomlinson sustained my position + Pres Smart endorsed same. Said, just as sure as the law of our temporal salvation must be received and practiced—(United Order) just so sure must the law of our virtuous salvation (Plural marriage) be lived. They both will be returned to us. The Savior will not come until these laws are being lived up to.[23]

Despite the manifesto, public support for the practice was reasonably normalized at this time, adding to the ambiguity surrounding the end to plural marriage in 1890. At one Church meeting that involved new members of the religious community, Musser documented that the men "asked several questions and they pledged themselves to observe the Word of Wisdom, pay honest tithing, sustain the authorities, be exemplary in all things, and accept all the principles of the Gospel, the Principle of Plural Marriage being expressly mentioned and we were pledged to believe it and defend it at all times."[24] Such moments highlight the challenging period in which Musser and the other men of his Quorum found themselves. While the institution publicly condemned the practice, the internal dialogue among members and local leaders often proved counter to public statements.

Not long after marrying his second wife, Musser attended the Salt Lake City Tabernacle and heard Joseph F. Smith speak during the April 1904 meeting of the Church's General Conference. At the time of the conference, the Church was under heightened surveillance amid the Reed Smoot Senate hearings. Musser closely watched the Smoot case and heartily celebrated his victory. In 1907, Musser congratulated Smoot on his victory and corresponded with him briefly over the year. In one such letter, Smoot included an index of the court hearings:

> I haven't the exact figures as to what the investigation cost our Government, but I think it was something over forty thousand dollars. It is impossible to say how many signatures there were to petitions asking my exclusion or expulsion from the Senate, for thousands of them were never presented by Senators, but merely thrown in the waste basket; however, I believe that there were over a million of them.[25]

While Smoot was not a polygamist, he represented the nation's anxieties about a polygamous faith. His success in securing the Senate seat was a success not only for the Church but for polygamous Mormons who viewed the outcome as hopeful for their future place in the Church and nation.

The April 1904 General Conference was significant. During this meeting, Joseph F. Smith spoke the Second Manifesto from the pulpit, another official end to plural marriage. With the Smoot hearings expressing concern about the "Mormon problem," Smith's statement sought to set the record straight about the "numerous reports of the persistence of polygamy.[26] Musser's reaction, as found in his daily musings, was unremarkable. He simply wrote, "Attended closing day of conference. Saints voted unanimously to sustain the following statement presented by President Smith."[27] A newspaper clipping of Smith's statement and a comment on a committee called to erect a monument to Joseph and Hyrum Smith accompanied the entry. To say that Musser found the statement unworthy of further consideration would prove an understatement.

The mundane response to the statement again signaled the uncertain period that marked the turn of the century for many Latter-day Saints and foreshadowed Musser's future trajectory. Four days after the Second Manifesto, Musser spoke in the Tabernacle about the General Conference.

Among his most foreboding points, Musser "admonished the Saints to be wise and not scatter rumor or indulge in gossip regarding their neighbor."[28] The concern was not without cause. The new statement against polygamy and Musser's refusal to end his marriages became a spectacle in light of Smith's statements. Musser was a husband to two living women and the father of seven children. In the mind of many like him, who retained their plural family relationships, the separation of eternal sealing bonds forged by the priesthood was inconceivable. But the refusal to abandon the practice placed families at odds with neighbors and outsiders who increasingly derided the practice.

Against the counsel of senior Church leaders and the Second Manifesto, but in line with his religious convictions, Musser was sealed a third time to Ellis R. Shipp Jr. in 1907. The sealing occurred in the Musser home under the authority of Judson Tolman, at the recommendation of either Henry S. Tanner, Matthias Cowley, or Nathan Clark.[29] Tolman was ordained a patriarch in 1895 and sealed to six women over the course of his life, including two sealings shortly after the Second Manifesto, to Eleanor Odd William and Marie Forsman.[30] In his role as patriarch, he conferred hundreds of blessings and performed multiple plural sealings through an interpretation of *Doctrine and Covenants* 124:93 that favored the practice: "That whoever he blesses shall be blessed, and whoever he curses shall be cursed; that whatsoever he shall bind on earth shall be bound in heaven; and whatsoever he shall loose on earth shall be loosed in heaven."[31] (The LDS Church currently interprets these passages as the patriarch's power to seal blessings only, not marriages. The interpretation was clarified in Heber J. Grant's condemnation of the rogue practice during the April 1921 General Conference.[32])

Tolman's document that recorded Musser's fourth sealing does not specify which man authorized the marriage. It was, nevertheless, conducted under the authority of Church leadership. The divergence between public statements and private practice led many to question the nature of Church policy and revelation. Among them was Musser, whose refusal to comply with the Church's statements on polygamy shaped his later questioning of whether the manifesto was actually a statement on government compliance. At the time of the revelation, and in his reflections years later, Musser claimed that the Church's position was simply an attempt to protect Reed Smoot's political career and preserve Church assets.[33] Musser's reflections led him to publicly question whether the end of LDS plural marriage was a revelation or a change in Church practice merely to appease the public.[34]

Debate over the nature of the Second Manifesto did not negate its tangible impacts. The statement escalated Church discipline for individuals who practiced polygamy. Musser's first encounter with the disciplinary process occurred at a meeting on July 22, 1909, in the Salt Lake City Temple with the Quorum of the Twelve Apostles. After waiting more than an hour, he was received into the meeting by Francis M. Lyman. At the time, Lyman was the president of the Quorum.[35] The nature of the meeting was immediately striking. Several men in the room, namely John Henry Smith, Rudger Clawson, Heber J. Grant, and Anthony W. Ivins, had either solemnized plural marriages for others or married plural wives themselves after the Manifesto. The presence of these individuals made tangible the contentious nature of polygamy's final years and contributed to Musser's feeling that "the Quorum is not united, and that such actions as these will tend to lose them their influence among the Saints." In his longest journal entry to that date, Musser gave a detailed overview of the two-hour interaction, in which he was the "object of inquisition, to get information regarding the practice of Plural Marriage since the discontinuance thereof by the church; also to array those who are now favoring the practice."[36]

During the meeting, Musser was asked about President Joseph F. Smith's Manifesto, issued just five years prior, and whether he was aware of solemnized plural marriages after 1904. Of equal concern was whether Musser believed there was someone on the earth who held authority to perform plural marriages. He responded in the affirmative, believing President Smith held the sealing keys and supported new plural marriages in the postmanifesto era. In Musser's defense, Smith did cohabit with his plural wives after the manifesto and fathered a child with one of his plural wives during the Reed Smoot hearings in 1904.[37]

Central to Musser's defense was the Church's hierarchical order for discipline. Technically, the men who oversaw the day's questioning had no authority over his standing in the Church. Instead, he rightly argued, his stake president was the man with legitimate authority over his place in the Church. In a pointed response to the committee, he elaborated:

Now Bro. Musser, we want you hereafter to join with us in putting this thing down. If any body comes to you for information or encouragement, tell them it can't be done, that it is wrong to desire and that no attention whatever should be bestowed upon the sisters with this in view. Pres. Lyman, I can't do that, but I suggest if you have any instructions to give me, it should be done thru my stake President with whom I am in harmony and I will endeavor to remain so. This answer beat out quite an animated discussion on the subject of authority the brethren in the main contending that it was none of the business of the Stake Presidency what should be required by the General Authorities of individuals. I took the ground that instructions might be given by the apostles contrary to those received by my Stake President, in which event I would be justified in following counsel of the Stake Pres. and leaving responsibility with him. This position was sustained in fact as I brought forth illustrations but as pertaining to the present subject it was declared wrong.[38]

The Quorum conceded Musser's point on file leadership and the organizational structure of the Church, bringing an end to the meeting.

The meeting highlighted a stark reality. The Quorum of the Twelve, and the leadership of the Church generally, was divided over plural marriage, most clearly represented in the resignation of Matthias Cowley and John W. Taylor, found "out of harmony" with the Quorum, only three years prior to the July 22 meeting.[39] In Musser recounting,

> My own feelings are these: That the investigation along the lines it is being carried out, is unwarranted. That the Quorum is not united, and that such actions as these will tend to lose them their influence among the Saints. Bro. Grant said they were going to cut Bro. Higgs off the Church, and his tone and manner was vindictive. My impressions were that the brethren are not activated by the proper spirit. . . . I can't understand the attitude of some of my brethren, but am willing to leave all for final working out of our God, seeking to be an humble instrument in the hands at all times in doing good.[40]

The lack of uniform policy in Church discipline was made more apparent by the unlikelihood that a disciplinary hearing would come from Musser's stake president, William H. Smart. Smart was an unrepentant polygamist and intimately tied to Musser through Church service and business ventures. At the time of this meeting, the men long conspired to begin a consecration program and revive the United Order.[41] At the same time, the meeting confirmed an already lingering feeling that the men in the Quorum were acting out of emotion and vindication, not the welfare of the community.

Apostles Heber J. Grant and Francis M. Lyman found Musser out of harmony with the Church. Despite that outcome, there is no indication that he was disfellowshipped or excommunicated for his actions. With such outcome, Musser simply promised to "endeavor to be in harmony." Notably, in his appeal to retain his membership, he stopped short of a promise to change.[42] On the contrary, he wrote that he "could not promise what my future course might be in case new light came upon the subject."[43] By the end of the meeting, Musser became concerned with the Church's leadership and the institution's future direction. He was unshaken in his conviction, however, about plural marriage and the priesthood authority that solemnized their sealings. He resolved to continue his marriages and advocacy for the marriage system instituted by Joseph Smith, even under the threat of death, "I had a definite testimony of the sacredness and correctness of the principle of Plural Marriage, and hope to be prepared to lay my life down for it if necessary."[44]

Excommunication and Ordination (1920–29)

Joseph W. Musser's appearance before the Quorum of the Twelve Apostles in 1909 marked one of the final entries in Musser's available journals until he resumed his regular entries in 1920.[45] Little information on his life immediately after the meeting in the Salt Lake City Temple survives, but clearly the 1909 disciplinary hearing marked a decisive turn in Musser's life. His autobiography offers some insight into this period, notably an event in 1915 that solidified his position on plural marriage. Musser recalled that "In the year 1915 an Apostle conferred upon me the sealing power of Elijah, with instructions to see that plural marriage shall not die out."[46] He further explained, "President Snow had said I must not only enter the law, but must help keep it alive. This then, was the next step in enabling me to help keep it alive. I have tried to be faithful to my trust."[47] No contemporaneous records corroborate these events, but the 1915 instructions by "an Apostle" were central to the way Musser understood his place in the Church and foreshadowed the claim to priesthood authority that he developed later in life.

Musser's apathy to his disciplinary hearing became a concern in the following decade, especially as rumors circulated about his continuous interest in plural marriage. On February 23, 1921, Musser had a conversation with

President Franklin Y. Taylor that reflected these concerns and an upcoming case against him before the High Council:

> Had a talk with Pres. Frank Y. Taylor regarding my case before the High Council. It seems I have broken faith with the "Woodruff Manifesto" and have taken more wives than one. Many have done likewise, but some earlier than I am up before the High Council. I have 19 children, most of whom I am supporting,—tho others taking care of themselves. I am serving about 70 meals a day and during this season of high cost of living! But they want my scalp, and will get it. Pres. Taylor is a Prince of a man—He is true blue, but the "system" demands my scalp and will get it! But I have done my best and I am not afraid of the outcome God's law will prevail, I know it and TIME will prove it! I told Pres. Taylor I had no defense, but that the law of the Church must take its course. And so be it.[48]

Musser did not deny the allegations against him but simply noted that others did the same with no consequences. Once again, the lack of uniform policy and procedure became a pointed complaint.

The High Council case occurred one month later, on March 12, 1921. The accusation against Musser was a suspected plot to marry a fourth wife, Marion Bringhurst. Not much is known about Bringhurst other than her family's opposition to postmanifesto plural marriage, a possible cause for convening the disciplinary council. Notably, the marriage never happened: In his own words:

> The facts are that Marion, who is vastly superior to the comon [sic] "herd" had indicated her believe [sic] in plural marriage to me and also that she felt she had found in me her chosen mate. I cheerfully responded to her sentiment and convinced her that the principle was right and proper even in this day. We had a common understanding that no ceremony had been performed, but I was tried for something that might have happened.[49]

Musser never married Bringhurst, either before or after the council. In the mind of his Church leaders, intent was enough to warrant discipline. When it came to plural marriage, the Church was concerned with correct practice *and* belief.

By the time of the council, Musser conceptualized himself as a sacrifice for the sake of renewed internal commitments to the changing public perception of the Church.[50] He recognized that the practice of polygamy was encouraged throughout his life, including by Lorenzo Snow, Wilford

Woodruff, and Joseph F. Smith. Even Heber J. Grant, the Church's most ardent opponent of plural marriage, was polygamously sealed to three women. Musser's lifelong Church experience emphasized the eternal nature of polygamous unions and their theological necessity. Polygamy was not only a practice but an enmeshed part of Mormonism. Musser could not untangle these realities in his mind.

Musser's appeal to history was not enough to save his membership in the Church. Ten days after his trial before the High Council, the notice of his excommunication appeared in the *Deseret Evening News*, a copy of which was neatly taped into his journal. He expressed hope that someday he would have the opportunity to stand before "Judges where Justice alone presides."[51] At the same time, he felt called to remain humble in light of the decision and determined to continue his faith. Although disillusioned by the institution, he never wavered in the foundational beliefs passed down from Joseph Smith. Always one to mingle the mundane with the extraordinary, the entry for the date of his excommunication ended with the simple phrase, "very busy at office."[52]

Musser believed he was a casualty in a new era of Church history that sought to finally "convince a doubting nation it was sincere in ending polygamy," as Marianne T. Watson noted in her work on the early years of the fundamentalist movement.[53] The period led many to question the motivation behind ending the practice. Among the possible reasons was Reed Smoot's election to the United States Senate in 1903.[54] To add to the controversy, Musser witnessed members of his local leadership testifying to the practice after his excommunication, which exacerbated his sentiment that he was a sacrificial offering. Two months after his excommunication, Musser attended the funeral for Aunt Lizzie Shipp. During the funeral, Elder George Gibbs, the secretary of the First Presidency of the Church, spoke and "bore testimony to the sacredness of the principle. It is eternal, and must be accepted for the blessings predicated upon it. Commended those who are keeping it alive and who are continuing in the faith of their fathers."[55] Musser was among the men "keeping it alive," at the expense of his Church membership.

Difficulty with the Church had only begun, and his ecclesiastical discipline coincided with an increase in family turmoil. The years after his excommunication offered a glimpse into the struggles many plural families faced in the twentieth century. Rumors about Church status and the faith of polygamous families were at the center of the tension. After his excommunication, Musser learned from Mary C. Hill that community members were speculating about the family's Church membership status. Some told his wife that the family would forfeit their blessings if she continued living in the Musser home.[56] He learned that a certain Grace Tout had "appointed herself a committee of one" to inquire about Musser's status in the Church.[57] In her quest for information, she "consulted with Apostle Jos. F. Smith Jr. who informed her that I had lost all my blessing and if my wives persisted in living with me, they would lose theirs including their children, who would, in eternity, be given to some one more worthy."[58] When he eventually wrote his autobiography, Musser recalled these moments as fervent persecution that followed him for his entire life.

Amid Musser's increasingly tense family affairs, the earliest iteration of the fundamentalist movement began. Nathaniel Baldwin, a Mormon inventor, was among the first to document the meetings of disenfranchised polygamous Mormons who lost their spiritual home after the Second Manifesto. At one such meeting, during a Sunday School class at a stake conference on August 21, 1921, Musser first encountered a community of families excommunicated for the practice of polygamy but ardent in their faith.[59] Among the attendees were John W. Woolley, Lorin C. Woolley, Israel Barlow, and Barlow's son, likely John Y. Barlow. Musser wrote, "Strong testimonies were born concerning the truth of the gospel and especially concerning the principle of plural marriage."[60] By the time of this gathering, Lorin C. Woolley was already making authoritative claims about the priesthood and plural marriage, as well as his authority to perpetuate both outside the confines of the LDS Church.

Woolley did not record a diary. Most historical information about the man was recorded by Musser in his journals or the minutes for the Woolley School of the Prophets, an organization of senior priesthood members that commenced on September 1, 1932, and operated until 1941.[61] During these meetings, Woolley expanded Mormon doctrine, and the earliest theological framework of the later fundamentalist movement emerged. In addition to his fanciful biographical information, Woolley taught revisionist narratives, including Theodore Roosevelt's conversion to Mormonism and entry into the Grand Council, after which Roosevelt accepted the "Patriarchal order of marriage" and received his endowments.[62] While there is no historic documentation for these claims, the Woolley accounts offered something that the men and women who gathered to hear his words felt lacking in the institutional Church. In Woolley's meetings, the windows of heaven were opened, and the possibilities were endless.

Among Woolley's early claims was a October 6, 1912, "Statement of Facts" about a catalyst event twenty-six years prior. In his statement, Woolley recalled an evening in 1886 when Church President John Taylor was "on the under-ground" amid heightened tension over the practice of polygamy.[63] As he retired for the evening, Woolley stood outside Taylor's door to keep watch. At 9 o'clock, voices that emanated from Taylor's room and a bright light woke Woolley. Morning dawned, the voices hushed, and the light dimmed. As Taylor emerged from the room, he shared that he met the spirit of the late President Joseph Smith and resurrected Jesus Christ, who offered instruction on the legal status of polygamy and whether Church leaders should provide a manifesto to end the practice.[64] After his eight-hour meeting with Smith and Jesus Christ, Taylor decided he would "suffer my right hand to be cut off before I will sign such a document."[65] The Woolley statement circulated widely among excommunicated Mormons, accompanied by the revelation given to John Taylor during the meeting. The revelation, colloquially referred to as the 1886 Revelation, proclaimed the irrevocable nature of covenants and eternal commandments. Those men who heard this message interpreted the revelation in the context of Taylor's political concerns and received its content as an assurance that God looked favorably on plural marriage.

Musser first encountered the 1886 Revelation on March 12, 1922, at a "special meeting" in Nathaniel Baldwin's home.[66] At this meeting, two hundred people gathered for six hours to discuss the status of their marital practice and polygamous families. Daniel R. Bateman, a later leader in the fundamentalist movement, stood and relayed the Woolley story, adding a prophecy that "the day will come when your brethren will handle you for trying to serve the Lord and keep his commandments for which we are in hiding today."[67] Already in 1922, a line was drawn that marked the polygamous families as persecuted for the sake of righteousness. In his recollections that evening, Musser included a copy of the 1886 Revelation with a simple comment: "Wife Ellis was at the meeting with me. She enjoyed it."[68] That same month, Musser attended a Sunday meeting with many of the same people who were present when he first learned of the revelation. This time, taking an active role in the meeting, he "bore strong testimony regarding Celestial marriage and the United Order."[69] Musser's involvement in these gatherings continued, many at the Baldwin home. On April 9, 1922, one month after his first meeting, Musser first encountered Woolley as the evening's speaker.[70] He was instantly captivated.

The April 9 meeting differed from previous ones that spoke of an additional revelation. At this meeting, Woolley revealed to the eager audience that he was "ordained an Apostle by President John Taylor and Geo. Q. Cannon."[71] To those who likely raised eyebrows at this claim, he simply asserted that "there are more Apostles out of the Quorum of Twelve than in."[72] The statement affirmed Musser's belief in a divided Quorum and his suspicion that some members of Church leadership were sympathetic to the growing polygamous movement. At the same time, the statement laid the groundwork for future claims of alternate priesthood lineage and authority to perform plural marriage. Along these lines, Woolley further claimed that he "had been directed to continue teaching the principle of Plural Marriage and encourage the people who are worthy to practice the same to the end that there shall never be a time when children will not be born under this covenant."[73] Woolley's claim came alongside a foreshadowing of a time when "we would be called to preside and hold leading positions in the church."[74]

Many of Woolley's claims were dubious, including the assertion that "he knew the Manifesto, because he helped to make it."[75] Because he stretched the truth in other matters, his recollection of significant historic events requires further interrogation. Nevertheless, no one at the Baldwin home contested Woolley's account of history or his position on authority. His story was one of the hardship polygamous Mormons experienced and provided leadership to a community removed from their spiritual home. He gave expression to their desire for a community of Latter-day Saints who preserved the faith in "one heart and one mind."[76] Under Woolley, the disparate families who lost their spiritual home solidified into an emergent movement.

As Musser became increasingly part of the movement, his temporal affairs deteriorated. Only three days after the meeting in the Baldwin home, he expressed frustration in his worsening financial difficulty. "Am awfully worried over financial situation. Busy at the office continuously and yet no money coming in to meet the many demands upon me. There seems to be little relief in sight."[77] Musser struggled with financial instability for most of his adult life, only exacerbated by his growing polygamous family. Although he received no formal education, he retained administrative work in the electric, water, oil, and real estate industries. "Routine day at office" became a common refrain that punctuated his diary entries. Despite his efforts, he continually borrowed money to meet expenses, was overdrawn at the bank, and faced various forms of debt with friends and colleagues. In moments of "sweating blood" over his financial precarity, he "cried out to God for deliverance."[78] Deliverance never came, and his financial distress was compounded with relationship turmoil and marital dissatisfaction.

Musser's belief in the practice of plural marriage did not amount to ease in its practice. On the contrary, his plural relationships were marked by hostility. Once willing to live the principle, by 1922, Rose became disillusioned with the practice and began "antagonizing" Musser for his marital choices.[79] Her antagonism manifested itself in increasing separation from the other families. As Rose grew more and more distant, Mary became disillusioned with both Musser and her marriage. Musser blamed members of the LDS community, who supposedly influenced her to denounce her marriage.[80] In one of his longest journal entries on his relationship with Mary, he recalled a meeting where Mary expressed her desire for Musser to no longer visit her. "She says the Lord has taken from her love from me and she does not desire me to visit her in future, but of course should have perfect liberty to see the children and to support them."[81] Nevertheless, Musser affirmed his love for Mary and his expectation to "lead her into the Celestial Kingdom of God."[82]

Musser's affirmation of love was not enough, and both women ultimately came together in their mutual dissatisfaction. Musser compared himself to the late Mormon founder Joseph Smith Jr. to understand his marital, professional, and relational turmoil: "I am in much the same position, of course on a smaller scale, but the principle is the same, as the Prophet Joseph Smith, when he crossed the river to come west, and escape the fury of the mobcrats, his friends, and especially his wife."[83] After years of struggle with plural marriage, Rose filed for divorce on January 2, 1946. She claimed desertion. Contrary to Rose's claim, Musser's recollections imply a continued love for one another, despite incompatibility. Unable to continue in the marriage, "she made it clear she did not want a temple or priesthood divorce; she wants our relationship to continue in eternity; and, of course, I am supporting her the best I can, as I have always done."[84]

Saint Joseph White Musser

Musser's tense family dynamic coincided with closer affiliation with his new religious circle. One such figure was John T. Clark, a man excommunicated from the LDS Church in 1905 over advocating polygamy, as well as over claiming authority as the "One Mighty and Strong."[85] In the Mormon fundamentalist movement, the One Mighty and Strong is mostly associated with Joseph Smith or is used by men to claim authority as God's elect.[86] In contrast with many other Mormon fundamentalist men, Clark never practiced polygamy. Priesthood authority, not polygamy, was what made fundamentalism appealing to him. *The One Mighty and Strong*, Clark's only circulated pamphlet, dictated to Musser in 1922, outlined this interest and his claim to authority.[87]

Through his relationship with Clark, Musser was introduced to Woolley's newly proposed priesthood history and the belief that a priesthood existed apart from the LDS Church to solemnize postmanifesto plural marriages. According to Woolley, "At the time Pres. John Taylor received his revelation in 1886, at his father's home. . . . Pres. Taylor said in substance: At the time of the 7th President of the Church, the Church will be in spiritual and financial bondage, and then the Lord will raise up a deliverer as spoken of in the 85th Sec. of the Doctrine and Covenants."[88] He continued, "It was at this time that Pres. Taylor placed his hands on his (Bro. Woolley's) head and ordained him an apostle and gave him a certain mission to perform with relation to Celestial marriage."[89] Within the context of the later fundamentalist movement, these Apostles were men appointed by God, rather than elected by the temporal Church.[90] Each testified that they met with the resurrected Jesus Christ and historical leaders in the Church who personally selected them for their role in the movement. Positioning the fundamentalist leadership as selected in a more elevated way than their LDS counterparts remained a defining feature of the movement for the remainder of its history.

By 1929, Lorin C. Woolley's statement on the 1886 Revelation accompanied an ordination claim that espoused priesthood offices outside the LDS Church hierarchy. That same year, Musser became intimately connected to this priesthood. On May 14, 1929, Woolley laid his hands on Saint Joseph W. Musser's head to offer one such ordination blessing. On that day, Musser wrote, "Received most wonderful blessing from Bro. Loren C. Woolley. Spent 2½ hours with him listening to his past experiences. I rejoice greatly. Vital points to be considered: Patriarch, Apostle, Family ties—Sustain-Saved, Great in Kingdom and Church, Humble, Wise."[91] Years later, in his autobiographical reflections, Musser reflected on the events of that day in greater detail: "I was ordained a High Priest Apostle and a Patriarch to all the world, by a High Priest Apostle, and I was instructed to see that never a year passed that children were not born in the covenant of plural marriage."[92] In addition to Musser, Woolley ordained J. Leslie Broadbent, John Y. Barlow, and Charles Zitting. Together with Woolley's father, John W. Woolley, the men constituted a priesthood organization that they called the Council of Friends, which they believed to be the most significant Mormon organization on earth.

The Priesthood Council (1930–54)

When Musser first heard Woolley declare that Apostles existed aside from the Quorum of the Twelve Apostles, he likely did not understand the implications. Then, only seven years later, he was one of them. In his later recollections of his standing in the Mormon cosmological order, he wrote, "It is strange that after being called to embrace the Patriarchal order of Marriage, I should be persecuted by my brethren for upholding the practice of it; that I should be cut off the Church, as they suppose they have done, and ostracized. They little know that under the ordination I have received—that of Apostle and Patriarch in the Kingdom of God—that I am the Church, insomuch as I remain faithful (see D&C, 84th Sec.)."[93] The ordination gave Musser renewed standing and elevated his position to equality with the men who ousted him from the institution.

Soon after Musser's ordination, on November 9, 1930, Mary succumbed in a battle with cancer. Musser eulogized her in his journals. "She faced life bravely and did what she conceived to be right. Her children beautiful, strong, and cultured as they are, are a lasting monument to the integrity and deep religious sense of the woman. She will live forever in the memory of God's faithful children. She is the only member of a large and prominent family, to receive celestial marriage in its fullness."[94] In the wake of his second wife's death, Musser found comfort in the community of his fellow polygamous believers, whom he frequently met for Church meetings, Sunday school, and conferences. Their support became increasingly important as the LDS Church escalated its actions against polygamists in 1931 under the presidency of Heber J. Grant, a once-polygamist LDS leader who became prominent in Musser's daily musings and frustrations because of his staunch opposition to the burgeoning polygamous movement.

The April 1931 General Conference marked a turning point in the LDS Church's stance against polygamy. For the first time, a Church leader used the pulpit to state the intent to support law enforcement in the effort to find and prosecute polygamists. As Musser recalled, "In opening, Prest. Grant delivered a written statement relative to the attitude of the Church on plural marriage, which gave nothing new, but caused much bitter comment."[95] The bitter feelings toward Grant did not begin during this conference but reflected decades-long frustrations with Grant's treatment of polygamous Mormons. For Musser, Grant's opposition was personal and included his interaction with Grant during his 1909 disciplinary hearing. Despite the renewed opposition to plural marriage spoken over the pulpit, Musser offered his testimony that "The purposes of the Lord will be accomplished in spite of the efforts of many of the people to thwart them. Patriarchal Marriage belongs to this dispensation—it is the law of the Gods—and it will never be wholly stopped. God will see to it that righteous men and women have the privilege of accepting it."[96]

Musser's awareness of Grant's statements reveals a broader trend about the fundamentalist movement, with significant theological implications. As Mormons, Church leadership remained on the radar of polygamists, who watched General Conference and believed that the LDS Church was the temporal institution of the Restoration. By the same token, they could not denounce the practice that cost their membership and reputations in the Church.[97] Musser ultimately resolved this conflict through his pamphlets that posited a theoretic separation between the Church and the priesthood.

Days after President Grant's conference statement, Charles F. Zitting, a close friend and member of the burgeoning fundamentalist movement, was tried in the city court for unlawful cohabitation. "An apostle started the first of persecution," Musser alleged, recalling Grant's General Conference statements.[98] He further recalled President John Taylor, who prophesied a time when faithful members of the Church would face both governmental prosecution and persecution by their coreligionists for the practice of polygamy. Zitting's prosecution was a fulfillment of prophecy:

> Bro. Zitting is living a higher law of the Gospel. His good wives, virtuous and pure women, are mothers. This is an alleged crime and men supposed to be guided by the Spirit of Christ are attempting to penalize women for having children in the manner God designed they should. Looking

forward to this day. Pres. Jno. Taylor is said to have predicted that many would be handled and ostracized from the Church for living this divine law, and some may have to go to prison and even lose their lives in re-establishing it. The prison threat has begun and an Apostle has started it. Where, Oh where, dear Lord, will it stop? How long will you permit those claiming to be your servants to so degrade their callings? Please hasten the scene and bring about the redemption of Zion.[99]

Despite the imprisonment of his friend, the mounting opposition did not deter Musser. Shortly after Grant's comments and Zitting's prosecution, he married Lucile Ottilie Kmetzsch in 1932. Kmetzsch was a convert to the Church who arrived in Salt Lake City from Germany on January 14, 1923.[100] Her son emphasized in his recollection of his mother that as a young convert, "Mother had been taught that the fulness of the Gospel included the law of plural marriage; and that such a system was necessary for herself left no doubt in her mind."[101]

Kmetzsch's ardent belief in plural marriage led her to propose to Musser shortly after they met. The marriage was performed in confidence, with only close family in attendance. Only one year later, October 14, 1934, she delivered her first child.[102] Despite the joyous celebrations in the family, not all relatives agreed with the arrangement. Among those who disapproved was her brother, who notified local Church leadership shortly after learning about the sealing. For her sealing to Musser and promotion of polygamy, she was excommunicated on July 17, 1933. Musser believed the disciplinary action was a "religious crime," as there was "no better woman is to be found than Sister Lucy."[103] Lucy's excommunication did not deter most of her family's support. In addition to Lucy's sealing, she "led the way for gathering," and several of her sisters gained prominence through their marriage to early fundamentalist leaders, including Lorin C. Woolley and J. Leslie Broadbent.[104]

In addition to his widely documented marriages, Musser married another wife, likely in 1933. In September 1930, Musser began referring to interactions with Myrtle Anderson in his journals.[105] There is not much information about Anderson; her first husband appeared at a Woolley School of the Prophets meeting on August 1, 1935.[106] Her marriage to Musser is missing from the US census record and little information exists about her relationship with Musser and the fundamentalist movement. Musser stated on September 10, 1933, "Miss Myrtle Anderson received a blessing—Bro.

Zitting mouth."[107] While the journal entry does not explicitly refer to sealing, the following year, Musser began to refer to Myrtle as another wife, "Wife Myrtle came from Wyoming, and had her in canyon for an outing yesterday. She remains staunch and true."[108] This marriage, like Musser's others, did not last. She eventually moved to Colorado and remarried. Despite her unhappiness in the marriage and in the movement her husband eventually led, some of Anderson's descendants remain active in Mormon fundamentalism and polygamous marriage.

The air of celebration around Musser's growing family halted in 1933 when President Grant again took to the pulpit and offered the Church's final statement on polygamy, retrospectively referred to as the Third Manifesto by Mormon fundamentalists.[109] Grant took a stringent position on the continuation of polygamy and was specifically concerned that the continual national speculation was "maligning the leaders of the Church."[110] For Grant, the continuation of polygamy was as much a matter of reputation and embarrassment as a matter of policy and obedience. In response to the continuation of the practice and its impact on members and leaders of the Church, Grant offered his final statement. The official statement addressed several key points, including the definition of marriage as a monogamous union and the fundamentalist claim of priesthood authority outside the LDS Church.[111] What made Grant's statement different from previous ones was his call to action, which required Church leaders to seek out individuals who were unwilling to comply:

> As persistent reports are coming to us of activity by a group said to be propagating a false doctrine and illegal practice of polygamous or plural marriage [sic], (the group apparently being composed of avowed or virtual apostates from the Church, of persons excommunicated from the Church, and of a few misguided but otherwise faithful members of the Church) we have deemed it wise to issue, under date of June 17th, 1933, and by way of warning and exhortation, an Official Statement which calls attention to the activities of that group, and which points out that neither the group nor its activities are in any way connected with the Church, that not only are the activities unauthorized and therefore illegal and void, but that they are contrary to the rule of the Church and the will of the Lord as revealed through President Woodruff and adopted by the Church, and that marriages performed by members of this group are false and mock marriages.[112]

A passive approach to the growing number of polygamists was no longer an option. In response, Grant exhorted local leaders to act:

> Any Church member belonging to this group or adopting or advocating its doctrines and practices is not to be considered in good fellowship in the Church, is not entitled to and should not be granted any of the rights and privileges appertaining to Church members—such as entry into the temples, the payment of tithes, participation in the activities of the priesthood quorums or of the auxiliary organizations of the Church, or in other Ward, Stake, or Church activities—and should, unless now truly repenting, be immediately and formally dealt with by excommunication, as directed in the Official Statement.[113]

Whereas one could believe in plural marriage and retain Church membership before 1933, despite more frequent excommunications after 1909, Grant's statements ended the decades of ambiguity.

Shortly after Grant released his statement on plural marriage, Diamond Oil Co. fired Musser from his position at the company. At the time of his termination, he had worked at the company for eleven years in various managerial roles. On the date of his termination in his journal, Musser included a copy of his termination notice and his suspicion of the reason: "I am a member of an oath-bound (by reputation) gang spoken of in the recent article of the 1st Presidency, and am making a business of marrying girls and inducing others to do like-wise. And since the Church is against me, I am a hinderance to the progress of the Company."[114] The termination confirmed Musser's early fears about the rumor mill in local congregations and their tangible impact on families. He further speculated, "I am charged with a moral and religious crime. Without a hearing or trial of any kind not even an opportunity to make an explanation, action is taken. I am deposed! How like the actions of Lucifer that is! Satan is behind ft [sic] all."[115]

The financial difficulty that Musser found himself in differed from his usual ones in that his termination coincided with the collapse of the American financial market and bank closures. His financial hardship and the failing monetary system in the United States, which he interpreted as a sign that warranted national repentance was the catalyst for his fervor to reimplement the United Order, Mormonism's nineteenth-century communitarian program. The urgency was amplified by his growing family and the addition of multiple marriages. Polygamy took an economic toll on families, causing early fundamentalists to argue that plural marriage required the United Order and a reconsideration of economic life.

Without immediate employment, Musser began "publishing the truth."[116] On August 8, 1933, he wrote the introduction to what became *Truth* magazine, a publication that reprinted the writings and lectures of Church leaders and added Musser's own editorials.[117] In the magazine, first published on the 143rd anniversary of Brigham Young's birth, Musser outlined the "fundamentals," which addressed political, social, economic, and spiritual reality.[118] Shortly after the project began, Musser sought counsel about his finances and debt from Lorin C. Woolley, the man who became a prophetic figure for many members of the fundamentalist movement. Woolley affirmed that Musser had a calling to ministry:

> Friday last I took up with Lorin the question of why since beginning to write my book, I had not been able to succeed along financial line. I had not only lost my job, but had failed in every undertaking to date. He said it is because your services are wanted in the ministry, writing and talking, and the Lord doesn't want you mixed up in other things that will detract your attention from your real work. I asked how I was going to get money to publish the book. He said the Lord had approved of it and means would come. I had already been impressed along these lines, but my natural reluctance to swim out in the deep waters made me hesitate. However, I resolved, and so told the Lord, to make his work paramount and all else secondary and asked him to assist me with means.[119]

Musser interpreted Woolley's counsel as a call to full-time ministry, which manifested in two decades devoted to the promulgation of fundamentalist history and doctrine. The pamphlets produced under Truth Publishing Company transformed Musser from an excommunicated member of the LDS Church to the most cited and prolific fundamentalist intellectual force of the twentieth century. Through his writings, a disparate movement became a cohesive faith community and a viable alternative for polygamous Mormons seeking a spiritual home.

As Musser moved forward with his ministry endeavor, he faced difficulty at home again. Only a few days before Woolley approached Musser for the ministry, Ellis expressed her dissatisfaction with the family's involvement in the fundamentalist movement. At this point, Ellis was the only wife who participated in Musser's new religious community. Her most

significant concern was Musser's opposition to the Church, which contra-
dicted her desire to "get in harmony with Church standards," something
Musser increasingly disparaged.[120] She also worried that association with
Musser would affect her son's ability to obtain future government employment.[121] Hostility only increased until March 12, 1934, when Musser and
Ellis separated. He wished her well, offered a blessing, and hoped for future
reconciliation. "Bless her for what she has been to me and may she be
preserved to do much good yet. And may the time come when through
a clearer light and a better policy of life, we may again be united, but in
a more enduring union."[122] In the following years, Ellis's feelings became
only more overt, and Musser lamented that Ellis did not want him in her
home and found his work "obnoxious."[123] He continued to blame outside
influence, and the two never reconciled. By 1934, Musser's early marriages
were over.

Musser published his first full-length doctrinal pamphlet in October 1933. Printed as *The New and Everlasting Covenant of Marriage,* the
pamphlet circulated in one hundred copies, some mailed to the General
Authorities of the LDS Church. At the same time, Musser began an in-
depth study of the priesthood, especially its relationship to polygamy. The
pamphlets portray the interconnected nature of the two subjects. Polygamy
was "priesthood marriage," and priesthood necessitated polygamy as the
"Patriarchal Order of Marriage." As long as the priesthood remained active
on the earth, Musser argued, polygamy would do the same through the
faithful dedication of a select group of men ordained for the cause.

The focused study on polygamy and priesthood coincided with the death
of Lorin C. Woolley, which solidified Musser's resolve to circulate the movement's ideas. Eulogizing Woolley's September 19, 1934, death, Musser wrote,
"God summoned home the President of Priesthood and he held Keys to
the Patriarchal Order."[124] He continued, "I can think of no man during the
past quarter of century [*sic*], in mortality, that has done so much toward
establishing and keeping alive the Patriarchal order of Marriage, and while
he is little known and less thot of by the present leaders of Ephraim, the time
will come when it will be seen he is high up in the councils of Joseph Smith,
Brigham Young, John Taylor, etc."[125] With Woolley's death, the sealing keys
passed to his second elder, J. Leslie Broadbent. Under Broadbent's leadership, the fundamentalist Mormon community steadily grew, supported by
the increase in LDS excommunications. In many ways, the organizations

maintained a symbiotic relationship throughout the 1930s. Both movements defined themselves in relation to the other and built their modern identities using the other as a foil.

Any possibility of rapprochement receded when J. Leslie Broadbendt died after a brief struggle with pneumonia on March 16, 1935. Musser oversaw the funeral and used the opportunity to speak on plural marriage and testify to its everlasting importance. Broadbent's passing marked the death of Musser's priesthood leader and longtime publishing partner. With Broadbendt's death, the senior member of the priesthood council, John Y. Barlow, rose to prominence. During Barlow's tenure, increased animosity against polygamists became the rule, including the formation of committees to search out those who continued the practice. Amid rising fear within the polygamist movement of the institutional LDS Church and mounting government surveillance, John Y. Barlow sent Ianthus W. Barlow, Joseph Lyman Jessop, and Carl E. Jentzsch to Short Creek, Arizona, to search for a place to establish a home for the polygamous community. Musser hoped the Short Creek settlement would be a catalyst for establishing the United Order, a consecration program Musser felt was necessary to faithfully live plural marriage. The settlement became a reality, but it also became a point of tension among the leadership.

The arrival in Short Creek was not easy. Legal prosecution escalated; nine people were charged with unlawful cohabitation: seven men and two women. Two of the men, Price Johnson and Isaac Carling Spencer, were prosecuted and the others were released.[126] At the time, about sixty families lived in Short Creek.[127] County Attorney Elmo Bollinger explained, "Officials of the regular ("Mormon") Church, were assisting to bring about the arrest and conviction of polygamists."[128] To Musser's dismay, "Church money is pledged to assist in persecuting the Saints."[129] Heber Grant's involvement in the prosecutions was formally expressed in a letter to Musser that concerned Charles Zitting's plural wife, Elvera C. Olson Zitting. Grant wrote, "I shall rejoice when the government officials put a few of these 'best bloods,' as you call them, in the county jail or the state penitentiary."[130]

For Musser, the LDS Church was to blame for the hostility that led to the Short Creek arrests and the greater antagonism that many polygamists felt in their LDS communities. LDS culpability was solidified with the implementation of loyalty oaths under Grant, which Musser published in *Truth*. The simple oath affirmed as follows:

Short Creek, Arizona Sept. 7, 1935.

To the Stake Presidency and High Councils of Zion Park Stake and To Whom It May Concern:

I, the undersigned member of Short Creek Branch of the Rockville Ward of the Church of Jesus Christ of Latter-day Saints, declare and affirm that I WITHOUT ANY MENTAL RESERVATION WHATSOEVER, SUPPORT THE PRESIDENCY OF THE CHURCH, and that I repudiate any intimation that any of the Presidency or Apostles of the Church are living a double life, and that I repudiate those who are falsely accusing them, and that I denounce the practice and advocacy of plural marriage as being out of harmony with the declared principles of the Church at the present time.[131]

The oath, in compelling the faithful to abandon the truth and accept false doctrine in Musser's belief, solidified his opposition to the Church and its leaders. In total, twenty one community members refused to sign the oath, leading to their excommunications. Although the number of fundamentalists who refused to sign was low, they represented the Church's inability to manage the growing fundamentalist community at Short Creek on the Arizona Strip. The LDS Church withdrew from Short Creek, disbanding the small branch and ward that the polygamists on the Utah–Arizona border had been attending.

As early as 1936, members of the fundamentalist movement were growing concerned about John Y. Barlow's "disposition toward one-man rule" over both the spiritual and the temporal affairs of the community.[132] Worried about mounting division in the community, Musser met with Barlow to suggest he focus on the spiritual matters of the community, leaving managerial concerns to other members of the council. Musser took the opportunity to ask Barlow how he viewed his position in the priesthood:

Thursday, Lewis and I had a personal talk with Bro. John Y. Barlow. We pointed out our fears that under the present setup the group could not prosper; that there seemed a disposition toward a one-man rule; that many of the Saints were complaining; that the present arrangement was not in accordance with the spirit of the action of the Priesthood recently taken, whereby it was advised that Bro. Barlow resign from the Management of the affairs of the group and confine his labors more particularly to the spiritual field; that our work was especially along the line of keeping faith in patriarchal marriage alive, and not in the directing of colonizing. Bro. Barlow was asked if he claimed to hold the keys of Priesthood, which he answered in the negative, saying, however, that he had dreamed of a personage coming to him and handing him a bunch of keys, and leaving without explanation. He did not know that that had any special significance. A meeting of the Priesthood was arranged for the following morning.[133]

Despite the question of whether Barlow maintained the authority necessary to oversee the spiritual matters of Short Creek, Musser maintained that Barlow's seniority was enough to grant him a presiding role that warranted support.[134] Nonetheless, he simultaneously affirmed that the survival of plural marriage was the primary function of Barlow's leadership and that all temporal affairs were outside his jurisdiction, despite his forceful position over the emerging communitarian organization, the United Trust.

The United Trust, named the United Effort Plan (UEP), became a source of hope and frustration for Musser. While he believed that communitarianism was necessary for families living plural marriage, its implementation within the council was a source of division. Barlow's heavy-handed one-man rule led to complaints from the Mormons in Short Creek.[135] In 1942, the United Effort Plan emerged as an effort toward communitarian living. Of the council, Louis Kelsch, LeGrand Woolley, and Charles Zitting did not join because of their belief that Short Creek needed to focus on plural marriage and not get caught up in other matters. Given this division, Barlow added Leroy S. Johnson and Marion Hammon to the council. The vote for these men was not unanimous; both Kelsch and Woolley abstained. From its inception, the United Trust incited schism and led senior members to question the direction of the community they built. The abstentions and decision not to join the program foreshadowed more profound divisions among the priesthood members.

During the implementation of the UEP, Musser remained in Salt Lake City and Barlow resided in Short Creek. With Musser absent, the signs of division became increasingly apparent. At this time, Barlow added Rulon Jeffs and Guy Musser, Musser's only faithful son, to the council. The addition brought the council to nine members, a significant shift in precedent from the initial five. Founding members were increasingly left behind as Barlow installed men loyal to himself to the highest leadership positions. Loyalty to the UEP became a hallmark of Barlow's leadership—refusal to sign a property lease from the UEP led to expulsion from the communitarian system by the council. Simultaneously, Barlow was implementing placement marriage, a system by which all marriages required priesthood approval for validation. Barlow's decision set a precedent for future marriages in the Short Creek community. In the years after Barlow's death, the system became especially controversial under the leadership of both Rulon Jeffs and his son, Warren Jeffs, who placed increasingly younger women with older men.

Musser's journals became sparse in the last decade of his life. The period coincided with his March 7, 1944, arrest along with forty-four other polygamist Mormons. The following year, Judge J. Allen Crockett of the Utah Third District Court sentenced fifteen men to a five-year sentence for unlawful cohabitation and conspiracy to promote unlawful cohabitation. Officers booked the men into Utah State Prison in Salt Lake City, where they were esteemed as ideal inmates. With the Short Creek community leaders in prison, Barlow devised a plan to speed up the release of the imprisoned. The plan, a pledge to align with the state on plural marriage, caused division among the men who read the document as a surrender to the government, not unlike the surrender they saw in 1890 among the leadership of the LDS Church. After much debate, Musser became one of ten who signed without the intention to live up to his signature's promises:

To whom it may concern:

The undersigned officers and members of the so-called Fundamentalist religious group do hereby declare as follows:

That we individually and severally pledge ourselves to refrain hereafter from advocating, teaching, or countenancing the practice of plural marriage or polygamy, in violation of the laws of the State of Utah and of the United States.

Saint Joseph White Musser

The undersigned officers of the religious group above referred to further pledge ourselves to refrain from solemnizing plural marriages from
and after this date contrary to the laws of the land.

JOHN Y. BARLOW
I. W. BARLOW
J. W. MUSSER
ALBERT E. BARLOW
A. A. TIMPSON
R. C. ALLRED
EDMUND F. BARLOW
JOSEPH LYMAN JESSOP
OSWALD BRAINICH
DAVID B. DARGER[136]

His signature granted Musser his freedom after serving only seven months
in prison. Zitting and Kelsch's decision to remain in prison and not bow
to the government's demands created a lasting strain on their relationship
with the other members of the council.

Soon after his release from prison, Musser suffered a stroke and was
placed under the care of Dr. Rulon C. Allred, a naturopathic chiroprac-
tic physician born to a polygamist family in Colonia Chihuahua, Mexico.
Although he joined the LDS Church as a teenager, he became disenchanted
with the institution after careful consideration of his father's published
defense of plural marriage, *A Leaf in Review*.[137] Musser's illness caused
concern and questioning arose about his ability to lead the fledgling religious community. Then Barlow died and left Musser as the senior member
of the council. As the new leader of the movement, Musser proceeded to
ordain additional members to the council, including Margarito Bautista
of the Third Convention, an organized group of Mexican Mormons who
expressed frustration over a lack of local governance in the Church, as
an Apostle and Patriarch.[138] In addition to Bautista, Musser ordained his
physician, Dr. Allred. The decision to go under the medical supervision of
Allred and subsequently ordain him into the Priesthood Council, became
one of the most decisive moments in Mormon fundamentalist history and
led to the most consequential schism in the priesthood organization.

Despite concern within the council, Allred's ordination was not without
good reason. Before the ordination, Allred had been an active member
of the fundamentalist community. In 1935, John Y. Barlow commissioned

Allred to perform sealings in California. In one of his wives' recollections of the blessing, "Joseph W. Musser had Rulon [Allred] stand with his shoulder next to his own right shoulder, Joseph standing a bit in front, and he told Rulon: 'You stood in this position next to me in the Spirit World, and you will occupy this position in the future.'"[139] The blessing was followed shortly after by Allred's commission to perform ordinances in "Idaho and elsewhere" under Musser's authority.[140] Finally, before his ordination in 1950, from 1947 to 1948, Allred was sent to Las Parcelas, Chihuahua, Mexico, as a missionary for the movement. While in Mexico, Barlow visited the Allred family and authorized Allred to "perform sealings and to keep the principle alive in all the world, and that he would not have to go to his brethren for direction but could act for himself under the direction of the Spirit of the Lord; that he was subject to no man's authority except his (that is, John's)."[141]

Despite his active involvement in the movement and leadership positions bestowed on him by the two most senior members of the Priesthood Council, the speed at which Allred accelerated in the priesthood hierarchy was unprecedented. In 1940 he received a Patriarchal Blessing from Musser that alluded to his future standing in the movement: "You shall have the power and the gift of a Prophet and a Seer and a Revelator and the Fullness of the Priesthood. The fullness of the Orders of the Priesthood will come to you and you will have the hands of your Savior laid upon your head."[142] His ascent within the hierarchy culminated on September 18, 1950, when Musser invited Allred to his home to receive a special blessing. The blessing was brief but carried lasting significance for the religion. "Brother Rulon C. Allred, by virtue of my Apostleship, I lay my hands upon your head and set you apart to be my First Counselor and to stand at my side as Hyrum stood to Joseph and as Leslie stood to Lorin, and I do this because the Lord has directed it, in the name of Jesus Christ, Amen."[143] The following month, on October 29, 1950, Musser presided over a Church night meeting and announced "he had chosen a counselor to himself and that man was Rulon C Allred. He was to counsel with him, take charge in places throughout the world where he (Jos) was unable to be, & act in his behalf just as though it were he himself."[144]

With this blessing, Allred effectively became the most powerful man in the community, bypassing Musser's son, despite a lack of seniority. In later accounts of Allred's ascent, his firm conviction of polygamy's necessity

34

became a defining feature of his position, which Musser acknowledged at the Thanksgiving Day 1950 announcement of his successorship:

> Brother Lorin C. Woolley told us that a man who could get and keep seven wives in full harmony with him was entitled to a seat in the highest Priesthood Council on earth, and also would be a King and a God. He said that a man with five wives in harmony would be entitled to be a prince and to be President of the Church, and a man with three wives so in harmony was entitled to the fullness of exaltation. You have seven wives in full harmony (he said to Rulon) and because of this and other qualifications, you are entitled to the blessings promised and you shall realize them if you continue in your present course until we go home.[145]

Much like Barlow's later ordinations, members of the council disagreed on whether Musser had the authority to place a man on the council without the unanimous consent of other members. Allred's ordination bypassed senior members, one of whom was Charles F. Zitting, a member of the original council ordained by Lorin C. Woolley, amplifying concerns. Once again, senior members who laid the foundation for the community were bypassed for someone in close personal proximity to leadership. The ordinations also fit the historic memory current leadership sought to cultivate.

When members of priesthood leadership cast their final votes, many refused to sustain Allred's ordination and his position as an Apostle, calling Allred's role as Musser's successor into question. Musser was unfazed by dissenting voices and presented Allred on May 6, 1951, as a "Patriarch in the High Priesthood."[146] The extent of the ordination's contestation cannot be overstated. Of the members of the council, only Rich Jessop sustained the ordination. Guy Musser, Musser's son who was added to the council by Barlow, argued that his father was mentally unfit and incapable of making decisions about significant leadership matters. He further argued that Allred used Musser and that, before his illness, both Musser and Barlow "put the members of the Council under covenant . . . to never accept Rulon C. Allred as an Apostle, that he was an aspiring man."[147] For that reason, he refused to sustain his father's successor and represented the council in their united front against the ordination. Joseph Musser remained firm in his decision, and Allred became a successor of the fundamentalist movement.

Saint Joseph White Musser died on March 25, 1954. To commemorate his life, *Truth* published a full-issue memorial for its late editor, complete with a biography, highlights from his editorial days, and statements from the men who knew him well.[148] Included was a letter from Musser outlining his will for his eventual funeral, including the use of the hymns "O My Father," "True to the Faith," and "Come Come Ye Saints." Thinking forward to his death, he indicated the desire for a simple funeral with close friends gathered to pay their respects: "I hope when I die I will go where the Lord intends me to go. . . . I love my friends and I testify that the Gospel is true—all of it."[149] Of course, the simple funeral he had in mind did not become a reality. His son, now editor of *Truth*, recounted, "Upwards of a thousand crammed the mortuary to attend his funeral services."[150] Musser's son reminisced on the work of his late father and leader and eulogized,

> Now that Saint Joseph White Musser has passed beyond the veil, what can be said of his life and labors? No doubt, it can be summed up in the following tribute: 'His passing marks the end of an epoch of the history of the great Latter-day Work. Who can calculate the effects his works had in the lives of his fellowmen? I am overwhelmed when I consider how great his works have been in my life and the people I know personally. I can visualize a glorious re-union on the other side where his works and effectiveness will be amplified.'"[151]

After Musser's death, Allred assumed the office of president of the priesthood and held authority over the polygamous Mormons from his home in northern Utah. His distance from Short Creek and controversial ordination proved too much for the community. Those who did not sustain Allred continued to follow the old council. The resulting division constituted one of the most significant splits in the fundamentalist movement, which eventually resolved into the Apostolic United Brethren under Rulon Allred and the Fundamentalist Church of Jesus Christ of Latter Day Saints under Leroy S. Johnson, John Y. Barlow's successor in Short Creek. In addition to these two large groups, Louis A. Kelsch and those who disagreed with the expanded role of the fundamentalist community continued to perform plural marriages independent of a council affiliation. With Musser's death, the already fractured movement was never again united.

One of the lasting questions within the fundamentalist movement is the extent to which Musser transferred his authority to other men in the community. Musser's second anointing in 1899 offered him unique standing in the movement as the only known member of the Woolley council to receive such an ordinance. The ordinance also placed him in a unique position relative to the institutional LDS Church, as someone assured exaltation in the eyes of the institution despite most subsequent actions. Musser's diaries offer brief evidence that he did offer this blessing to others and expanded the ability of numerous men to perform sealings. Musser wrote in a 1940 journal entry, "Attended general meeting at home of Bro. Zitting 6 P.M. and spoke on authority and general duties of Saints. Lucy performed beautiful ordinance of sacred nature."[152] Musser's account of Lucy's involvement in the 1940 ordinance implies the sacred event of that day was a second anointing ceremony, which conferred priesthood authority to participants. It is yet to be determined the extent to which Musser offered second blessings and, therefore, the full scope of the Mormon fundamentalist movement.

In a time of significant change in the LDS Church, Musser's life is an exemplary account of a Mormon who disagreed with the Church's response to modernization. Modernity succeeded in shaping twentieth-century Mormonism, a reality that continues into the present. The end of plural marriages in 1890 and 1904, and the subsequent excommunication of dissenters, allowed Mormonism to become a fully American religion and participate in a version of modernity that aligned with Protestant norms. Nevertheless, despite efforts to shape Mormonism into the image of its "right religion" counterparts, the things that made Mormonism notorious in the nineteenth century did not disappear, nor did the notoriety of its adherents. Musser's life and Mormonism offer a glimpse of an alternate way to enact modern Mormonism.

CHAPTER TWO

The Order Pertaining to
the Ancient of Days

> We have learned that a man may be President of the
> Church and not President of Priesthood, and not even a
> Prophet; that when the Church is set in order the President
> of Priesthood will be the President of the Church.
>
> —Saint Joseph White Musser, "The Priesthood's
> Supremacy," *Truth* magazine, July 1936

In 1933, Joseph W. Musser wrote his first full-length publication on plural marriage with polygamist sympathizer, J. Leslie Broadbent. Musser and the men of the Priesthood Council believed they were the avenue for the continuation of plural marriage, making polygamy the most pressing matter in the minds of its members. Because of the practice's discontinuation in the LDS Church, justification for plural marriage required a theological explanation to support its continuity and the fundamentalist authority to solemnize plural marriages. Therefore, it is unsurprising that Musser's exposition on plural marriage coincided with an in-depth survey on the priesthood, a topic that occupied much of Musser's writing. He did not dismiss or invalidate the long-standing priesthood history in the LDS Church that posited an unbroken line of authority from Joseph Smith to Heber J. Grant. Instead, his pamphlets argued for a higher priesthood that existed outside the temporal institution and acted as the avenue for plural marriage after the First and Second Manifestos.

The LDS Church teaches that the priesthood and the Church function in unison; the president of the Church acts as the president of the priesthood.

As the Church moved away from polygamy, Musser posited that the priesthood existed before the organization of the Church and has continued to exist independent of it. The priesthood's separation from an organizational structure allowed men with priesthood authority to act independently from the institution's jurisdiction. This hypothesis remains Musser's most significant and controversial contribution to Mormon thought. More than simply a justification for new theology, the evolution of this doctrine catalyzed hostility toward the Church and his religious dissent. Even today, his revisionist historical narrative informs the way many fundamentalists imagine their faith in relationship with the LDS Church.

In Musser's apologetic writing, his life became a tool necessary for upholding his extraordinary claims. Before his excommunication, Musser received his second anointing in the Logan Temple with his first wife, Rose Selms Borquist. While the theological implications and the practical availability of the ordinance changed significantly throughout Mormon history, the ritual incorporated Joseph Smith's theological innovation of a patriarchal priesthood and became synonymous with the "fulness of the priesthood."[1] According to the LDS Church, excommunication removes membership, dissolves ordinances, and revokes priesthood. Musser's participation in the second anointing called this standard practice into question. The ritual conferred the higher blessings of the priesthood and assured his exaltation into eternity. With this in mind, members of the early fundamentalist movement did not always accept the eternal consequences of Church discipline. They believed that the power of God remained present and operable in their lives despite disaffiliation from the Church.

God

The priesthood and its various manifestations are the center of Mormon religiosity. "As Priesthood is one of the cornerstones of the theology of the Latter-day Saints, it is incumbent on all Church members to give close and careful study to the subject," Musser affirmed in his introduction to the subject.[2] As the cornerstone of the faith, Musser argued that a correct understanding of priesthood underlies all other Mormon beliefs; every matter of doctrine and practice is a "priesthood issue."[3] To understand human experience, the nature of God, and the path toward exaltation, a correct recognition of priesthood is crucial.

Priesthood is "God's voice—God's power in the earth; it expresses the laws of the eternities, and is the power by which all earths are fashioned and ruled."[4] From the onset, this definition necessitated a concrete theology of God. Musser's pamphlet *Michael, Our Father and Our God: The Mormon Conception of Deity as Taught by Joseph Smith, Brigham Young, John Taylor and Their Associates in the Priesthood* laid the foundation for such a theology. First appearing in *Truth* magazine in 1937, the pamphlet rehearsed the character of Mormonism's embodied deity by reaffirming Brigham Young's teaching on the Adam-God doctrine. Using Young's controversial April 9, 1852, General Conference address as a starting point, Musser developed a Mormon cosmology that included a hierarchy of gods in an unbroken chain of priesthood that descends from the heavens.

In his April 9, 1852, sermon, Young asserted that the Archangel Michael descended into the telestial sphere and received a body. This body was Adam, the "the first of the human family" and the Ancient of Days.[5] According to Musser, Young was communicating special knowledge not contained in the biblical account. He likened the Genesis narrative to a "stork story," written for "the mental capacities of his [Moses] day."[6] Beyond the rudimentary tale contained in Genesis, Young was offering a more complete portrayal of the first people, their origins, and their fate. Within his expanded creation narrative, Adam and Eve's God, Elohim, created a world that He governed. Adam lived a life of obedience to the laws and commands of God. The reward for his faithfulness was translation, a return to God, and his exaltation in a celestial state.[7] In Young's account, Adam's wives were never far behind and similarly attained exaltation. Following Adam's footsteps, all men have the opportunity to serve their God, administer ordinances, follow the commandments, and become like God. The force that powers this process is priesthood.[8]

Recognizing the challenging nature of Young's doctrine, Musser made sense of its complexity through a hierarchical theology of "offices" and "titles" within the realm of the gods. He explained thus: "The key to understanding is the difference between the individual and the office held by the individual. 'God' is a title or office—a principle; and yet the being who occupies this office of God is an exalted man. The office of 'God' has always existed and always will exist. It, the office, is without 'beginning of days or end of years.'"[9] Regarding the world Musser inhabited, Michael holds the office of "God" and "Jehovah" became a salvific office for a deity who obtained a temporal body to redeem humanity. Jesus attained exaltation and resides among the gods because of his exemplary completion of this secondary office.[10]

Mortality was a central features of Brigham Young's cosmology. In his formulation of Adam as God, he broke with traditions that denigrated carnality by centering the body as the vehicle of exaltation. His departure from tradition presented a problem for conceptions of the Holy Ghost, the third member of the Godhead. Not one to leave loose theological ends, Musser used his theology of divine offices to embody the Holy Ghost as God's "witness to mankind."[11]

Like most of Musser's theological innovations, his theology of the Holy Ghost first appeared in *Truth* magazine. In a 1937 issue commemorating Smith, he wrote, "Joseph Smith's mission was that of a WITNESS, a TESTATOR. He came in the 'fulness of times,' to re-establish God's laws in the earth. Joseph's dispensation is the Dispensation of the Fulness of Times, when all things are to be gathered as one, never again to be taken from the earth."[12] The editorial did not make explicit what some likely saw in the statement. By this time, the phrase "witness and testator," used together, was used in reference to the Holy Ghost. In *A Compendium of the Doctrines of the Gospel*, Elder Franklin D. Richards and James A. Little wrote, "Everlasting covenant was made between three personages before the organization of this earth, and relates to their dispensation of things to men on the earth: these personages, according to Abraham's record, are called God the first, the Creator; God the second, the Redeemer; and God the third, the Witness or Testator."[13] The connection was clear for Musser. He simply connected the dots.

Years later, in his publication on the nature of God, Musser was less subtle. Drawing on his previous editorial and comments made by early Church leaders who raised questions about Smith's sometimes cryptic statements about himself, Musser considered another conclusion: "and why not Joseph Smith, who was the 'Witness or Testator,' 'God the third'?"[14] His question initiated a theological possibility that remains an active part of Mormon fundamentalist doctrine. Toward the end of his life, Musser became increasingly convinced that Smith's witness to the Restoration continued in eternity among the gods, and as one of them:

> Joseph Smith was one of the three Gods that were appointed to come here on earth and to people this earth and to redeem it—God, the Father, the creator; God the Mediator, the Savior, the Redeemer; and God the Witness and the Testator. Before they came here upon earth, and in the

presence of the great Elohim of this earth's galaxy, they entered into a covenant which established them as the Gods, or the Trinity of this earth.[15]

Priesthood and Church

Once Musser outlined the nature of God, Elohim's power became the subject of inquiry. Unlike his LDS counterparts, Musser focused his attention on what the priesthood is *not*; specifically, he insisted that the priesthood is *not* the Church. In his 1936 *Truth* magazine editorial, "The Priesthood's Supremacy," Musser sought to define priesthood and its central place in the entire history of humanity. It was a tangible reality passed down for generations and an indispensable part of the human experience.

> Priesthood is God; it is the power by which the Gods of eternity operate. It was by the power of the priesthood that the world was formed, that Enoch's city was taken up, that the flood covered the earth, that Mt. Zerin was removed by command of the Brother of Jared, that Jesus raised the dead Lazarus, walked on the water, stilled the storm, and finally laid down his body and took it up again. In the present dispensation, the Priesthood was restored to earth by John the Baptist and by Peter, James and John, acting in their respective callings.[16]

Mormonism's central claim is that the power of God was lost after the death of the original apostles and restored through Joseph Smith Jr. in 1829. As a Restorationist tradition, the Church's maintained that a "general apostasy developed during and after the apostolic period, and that the primitive Church lost its power, authority, and graces as a divine institution and degenerated into an earthly organization only."[17] On that basis, the LDS Church affirmed its mission as the "re-establishment of the Church as of old, in this, the Dispensation of the Fulness of Times."[18] If this basic historical claim is not true, according to James E. Talmage, "the Church of Jesus Christ of Latter-day Saints is not the divine institution its name proclaims."[19] Mormonism asserted that, along with alterations to Christianity's earliest doctrines and practices, the priesthood was removed from the earth. The situation changed on May 15, 1829, when two young men, Joseph Smith Jr. and Oliver Cowdery, knelt to pray and angelic messengers laid their hands on Smith's and Cowdery's heads, ordaining them to priesthood office.

Musser continued to develop this line of thinking in other publications. In *The New and Everlasting Covenant of Marriage, Supplement to the*

New and Everlasting Covenants of Marriage, and *Priesthood Items*, Musser offered a complete exposition of priesthood history, beginning with the prayer given by Smith and Cowdery. Assuming his readers were familiar with the LDS priesthood restoration narrative, Musser bypassed many details to highlight that the Church was not established when the men received the priesthood. After the ordination, they preached the Gospel, baptized converts, and manifested the gifts of the Holy Ghost, all under the auspices of the priesthood that "stood guard over God's people to warn, reprove, bless, console and direct."[20] All these actions happened in the absence of an organized church; therefore, the Church is not the priesthood but merely one arena where its powers are located. He concluded that "The Church being a product of the Priesthood—one of its tools, let us say—can properly function only as the Priesthood directs but, of course, the Priesthood can function independent of the Church and of all other subordinate organizations."[21]

The work of the priesthood eventually necessitated systematic organization, manifesting in the establishment of a Church where the priesthood operated in the lives of the faithful. The institutional Church became the framework for the operation of God's power:

> But the time came when further organizations were needed in order to advance the work more rapidly. One may, in time, build a house with the aid of a saw and a hammer, but better and quicker work may be accomplished with additional tools. The Church, with its complement of auxiliary helps, was the additional tool the Priesthood required at that time. It was accordingly organized with six members, Joseph and Oliver becoming the first and second Elders (its leaders) respectively.[22]

It went uncontested in Musser's writing that Smith held a primary place in the structure of the priesthood by virtue of his role in the Restoration of both the priesthood and the Church.

The LDS Church acknowledged two orders of priesthood, the Aaronic order and the order of Melchizedek. The Aaronic priesthood is a preparatory portion of the priesthood that grants men the ability to serve in various callings prior to their ordination to the higher order. This higher order, the Melchizedek priesthood, has the power to bless, baptize, and heal. Musser offered an alternate division to make sense of the separation between the priesthood and the Church. He named three orders, the Levitical priesthood that administers ordinances, the Patriarchal priesthood that oversees the Church, and the priesthood of the presiding elder, who acts as a prophet, seer, revelator, and translator.[23] According to this priesthood structure, the patriarch superseded the presiding elder in the Church, but not in priesthood. This role was historically aligned with Hyrum's position as patriarch, placing him at the highest organizational level in the Church. Joseph Smith, ordained to an order higher than Hyrum, became president of the priesthood.

To create further distance between the institutional Church and the priesthood, Musser identified a fourth, "additional," priesthood that was never institutionally organized.

> The Lord Himself handles this Priesthood and gives it to whom and when He pleases. Man does not call another man to this order, neither does man secure it by the request or selection of any man on earth. The call comes by messenger from heaven requesting designated individuals into the House of God (and it is what is known to Latter-day Saints as the second anointing), preparatory to receiving the Second Comforter, which completes their ordination. Sometimes this Second Comforter is given while in the Temple. Often it does not come until years after, even just at death. But they who have had their second anointings can see the face of the Lord and live, even though being in the flesh, as one sees and talks to another.[24]

This higher priesthood was part of Old Testament history, held by the patriarchs and Jesus Christ during his ministry on earth. It "governs and controls all the Priesthoods" and afforded holders the apostolic title.[25] The men who carried this priesthood in Smith's lifetime were members of a supposed Priesthood Council, or Council of Friends. To solidify the existence of this priesthood in the early LDS Church, Musser drew on sermons by Brigham Young, who spoke about the Melchizedek and Aaronic priesthoods and an "additional Priesthood that has never been delegated to the Church. The Lord Himself handles this Priesthood and gives it to whom and when He pleases."[26] The great prophets who served as heads of each dispensation held this priesthood. They included both Joseph Smith and Joseph Musser, by virtue of his second anointing and Woolley ordination, which made Musser an heir to the same authority.

Before his death, Joseph Smith ordained the Quorum of the Twelve Apostles to "all the keys and all the ordinances and Priesthood necessary for them to hold in order to carry on the great and glorious work of universal salvation."[27] In telling this history, Musser attributed new meaning to that event and implied that the newly ordained men did not previously hold that authority. In Musser's telling of priesthood history, the men in the Quorum were ordained to the Church's Melchizedek priesthood, but it was only immediately before Smith's death that they were initiated into a priesthood that extended beyond the earthly institution. The higher priesthood afforded the ability to seal families and forge eternal bonds that lasted into eternity. This priesthood, not the Church, is the one fundamentalists claim as their own.

In addition to the division between Church and priesthood, Musser wrote about a third division of God's power. The Kingdom of God, the third segment of the priesthood, was the basis for the world's governmental affairs, organized the Saints' lives, and acted as the foundation for plural marriage and United Order. The Kingdom of God was the basis for Brigham Young's dream of a theodemocratic nation in the Salt Lake basin and, later, Musser's vision for the Short Creek community. As the head of the Council of Fifty, the organizational structure that contained the third order of priesthood, Musser recognized Smith's primary position in both the Kingdom of God and the head of the priesthood.

While Musser traced his priesthood history from the life of Joseph Smith, it was not until 1929 that the fundamentalist movement superimposed Musser's history onto their movement. Their reimagined history began with recollections of a special meeting between the current president of the Church and his associates in 1886. According to later reminiscences of the evening, John Taylor, the third president of the LDS Church, retired to pray about plural marriage after discussing the federal government's escalated legal pressure against the Church. The men in attendance recalled a light emanating from Taylor's room as he prayed and voices emerging from the closed door. Taylor emerged after eight hours and explained an encounter with the resurrected Jesus Christ and Joseph Smith. During this meeting, culminating in the 1886 Revelation, or Eight Hour Meeting, Taylor confirmed the irrevocable nature of covenants and eternal commandments. Within the context of external persecution and the events that led to the meeting, Taylor's associates interpreted the revelation as an assurance that God would not "revoke" eternal covenants, understood as plural marriage specifically, rather than all covenants Latter-day Saints teach as essential.[28]

On the surface, the 1886 Revelation is about polygamy, but as Musser and other fundamentalists read it, it concerned authority to exercise the will of God on earth. The LDS Church's abandonment of plural marriage signaled that they had lost the power to govern God's kingdom on earth. Fundamentalists made this historical claim binding in 1922, when Lorin C. Woolley, one of the men present when Taylor received the revelation, stood before a crowd of Mormons sympathetic to the continuation of polygamy. He related his remembrance of the 1886 meeting and declared that he "had been directed to continue teaching the principle of Plural Marriage and encourage the people who are worthy to practice the same to the end that there shall never be a time when children will not be born under this covenant."[29] According to Woolley, John Taylor laid his hands on the heads of six men and ordained them to the office of High Priest Apostle, the highest order of the priesthood, with the power necessary to perform plural sealings outside the bounds of the Church. Following this logic, Woolley and the others ordained to the office of High Priest Apostle now superseded the LDS Church's priesthood authority and were authorized to witness and solidify new covenant relationships (plural marriages).

In 1929, Joseph Musser published the 1886 Revelation as an authoritative account of Lorin C. Woolley's 1886 remembrance, outlining Woolley's recollection of the event and creating a standard by which all other claims to priesthood authority would be judged. This account, published in *Supplement to the New and Everlasting Covenant of Marriage*, became the official history of September 27, 1886, for members of the fundamentalist movement. It circulated widely and initiated the broader apologetic aim of separating the priesthood from the Church. Believers, both fundamentalist and LDS, argue that, after Joseph Smith's ordination and the priesthood's restoration, the power of God would never again leave the earth, despite hell's full opposition. For that reason, the end of plural marriage, and other changes to LDS doctrine and practice, did not constitute another apostasy for the earliest fundamentalists.[30] The end of polygamy demonstrated the fallibility of temporal churches, not the fallibility of priesthood. The priesthood remained and independently contained the unchangeable teachings of God that were no longer part of the Church. While the LDS Church is the Church on earth, a higher priesthood perpetuated plural marriage.

Because the argument of priesthood's historical continuity was central to the fundamentalist movement, Musser sought to explain the existence of a priesthood council from the earliest years of the Church. To do so, Musser reimaged the early temple endowment as the place Joseph Smith instituted a special council of seven priesthood holders. Those men oversaw what Musser referred to as the Sanhedrin and held a higher form of authority than that accessible within the institutional Church.[31] On the day the Sanhedrin was initiated, on May 4, 1842, Joseph Smith, James Adams, Hyrum Smith, Newel K. Whitney, George Miller, Brigham Young, Heber C. Kimball, and Willard Richards met in the upper room of the Red Brick Store for instruction.[32] On that day, the men were ordained to "the order pertaining to the Ancient of Days" and granted "the fulness of those blessings which have been prepared for the Church of the First Born and come up and abide in the presence of the Elohim in the eternal worlds," known in popular Mormon discourse as "the Second Anointing."[33] Joseph Smith explained the event thus: "In this council was instituted the ancient order of things for the first time in these last days."[34] Musser, who had received this ordinance in 1899, saw himself in this historical event and harnessed it to articulate his position above the Church.

The combination of Joseph Smith's and Oliver Cowdery's 1829 ordinations and the later institution of the second anointing formed the primary arguments for Musser's vision of how the priesthood operated. To justify his position, Musser scoured the statements from early Church leaders in order to prove that these ideas had been present in Mormonism since its Restoration. Most notably, he became familiar with the *Journal of Discourses* to further his position, specifically as it related to priesthood and priesthood marriage. Orson Pratt's comments on the restoration of the priesthood were central to Musser's history: "The Lord, before He suffered this Church to be organized, gave authority to His servants to preach the Gospel and to organize His kingdom on the earth in fulfillment of the ancient prophecies."[35] The *Journal of Discourses* became a rich source of sermons that Musser perceived as the original teachings of the Church. Because the Church stopped citing the volumes and they were largely unread by members, they became useful to the fundamentalist position.

The doctrine of a higher priesthood offered a loophole to Musser and those who joined his movement. By dating the priesthood's restoration before the Church's organization, Musser articulated an apologetic solution for men retaining their priesthood once they lost their Church membership. By further citing the second anointing and its potential implications in his own life, he created a way for the fundamentalist movement to claim something outside the theological boundaries of the institutional Church. Even before his excommunication, Musser recognized the special authority he received through his second anointing, an authority higher than that of some of his leaders:

> Special Priesthood Meeting: Prest. Smith spoke of those invited to the meeting as being the best and highest standard of men in the church—the very kernel in the church. . . . We ought to rather loose [sic] our lives than to betray our brethren or the Kingdom of God. . . . Bishops are not supposed to know who receives 2nd anointing. It is the highest ordinance in the Priesthood and does not pertain to the Aaronic Priesthood."[36]

The fundamentalist movement's position on priesthood did not go unnoticed and sparked clarifying statements from the LDS Church, eventually correlated with changes to ordinance availability. After the April 1940 General Conference, *Truth* magazine gave special attention to Elder John A. Widtsoe's comments on the nature of the priesthood, which sought to counter the claim that the priesthood can exist independently from the Church. The LDS apostle conceded that "The Church derives its authority and power from the Priesthood which has been conferred upon it; Priesthood is its foundation."[37] Widtsoe assured listeners that the priesthood cannot function independently from the Church, despite its presence prior to the Church's organization. Musser responded that "The Saints should know that Priesthood is not a gift of the Church. It was the Priesthood that gave to the Church its organization, and that enables the Church to function as the Church of God."[38]

The second anointing was granted to Latter-day Saints far less often under the presidency of Heber J. Grant than under previous Latter-day Saint administrations. Before his presidency, several thousand second anointings had been offered in LDS temples by each president of the Church, with Lorenzo Snow authorizing two thousand, including Musser's.[39] Grant, contrary to previous trends, authorized only a few hundred. Grant's 1926 change in policy on the second anointing gives some explanation. Unlike previous times, when stake presidents had the authority to recommend the ordinance, Grant announced, "Second Blessings are only given by the President of the Church upon recommendation of a member of the Council of the Twelve."[40] Limited information is available about Grant's decision.

The rise in excommunications and men who used their ordinance experience to justify their standing outside of the Church, however, offer possible answers. At the time of the change, the Church needed to curtail dissent. Limiting institutional access to the fulness of the priesthood was a solution.

Priesthood Marriage

Musser's, Woolley's, and other fundamentalists' arguments about priesthood's definitions and authority were a microcosm of the growing tension between the polygamous movement and the LDS Church. Musser and his coauthor, J. Leslie Broadbent, viewed their reimagined priesthood history as inextricably tied to apologetics over polygamy.[41] While they conceded that the Church oversaw the basic Gospel message, their organization offered more. Musser clarified thus: "The two basic laws looking to our temporal and spiritual salvation, as set forth in the law book of the Lord, are the law of Consecration—United Order, and the law of Patriarchal marriage. . . . The law of plural marriage is the marriage law of the Priesthood and the only law recognized in the celestial heavens."[42]

In fundamentalist literature, polygamy was "patriarchal marriage," denoting the practice as part of the broader priesthood structure and distinct from nonmonogamy outside the Church. The interplay between priesthood and polygamy was widespread in Musser's writing, going as far as to argue that the destruction of the polygamous marriage system was a covert attempt to overthrow the priesthood. Referring back to the 1890 Manifesto, he explained, "It was not polygamy that the enemies of the Church were so anxious to destroy, but Priesthood."[43] Because of the connection that Musser saw between polygamy and priesthood, the "end" of LDS polygamy in 1890 was not simply a matter of abolishing a marriage system. It was about dissolving the Church's authority, and the attempt to preserve the practice was synonymous with assuring that the power of God remained present on the earth.

The connection between polygamy and priesthood became an apologetic tool to differentiate the Church from the priesthood. Musser's writing portrayed the 1890 Manifesto not as the product of divine revelation but as a political concession to an increasingly hostile government. The Church was "the propaganda division of the Priesthood," an auxiliary that allowed God's power to operate effectively.[44] The Church's purpose was to introduce the basics of the gospel and leave the higher ordinances and practices to the priesthood. In recognition of the Church's purpose, the men who published *Truth* accepted that the Church ended the practice of plural marriage without debate. Patriarchal marriage continued under the priesthood, however, and the Church did not possess the authority to stop the persistence of such marriages. The repudiation of polygamy was not a repudiation of the Church but of the power of God:

> "That I denounce the practice and advocacy of plural marriage, etc.", is not so easily answered. We would like to harmonize our faith and ideals with those of our file leaders could we do so without stultification. The question involves a principle of conscience, and to conform to the requirements of the Church means a repudiation of a faith and belief dearer to us than life itself. With us plural marriage is an eternal law to which ALL MEN must subscribe in order to regain the presence of their heavenly Father. It is a law of the Holy Priesthood; one that God himself, and His Son Jesus Christ, were forced to subscribe to and live. In the face of this belief, to "denounce" those adhering to this divine law, would amount to no less than a repudiation of our Lord.[45]

While the LDS Church ended the practice of plural marriage, the fact that new plural marriages were solemnized even in small numbers became another reason that Musser cited to demonstrate that God intended polygamy to continue outside the institutional Church. "That the Manifesto was not intended to stop polygamous marriages under Priesthood sanction is evidenced by the fact that the practice was not stopped," Musser wrote of the 1890 end to the practice.[46] Like Musser's other extrapolations of priesthood history, the fundamentalist movement drew on the early organization of the Church to justify the "secret" continuation of polygamy. Musser explained, "But neither in the days of Nauvoo, when the practice was confined strictly to the higher order of the Priesthood, or in the early days of Utah after the law became a church tenet, did the practice become general. Two per cent only of the Latter-day Saint population were credited with receiving and living the law."[47] The secrecy surrounding some early Mormon practices, including polygamy, furthered Musser's claim that the Church and priesthood were always separate.

In priesthood meetings, Musser argued that the Church was not prepared for some doctrines—which included the early years of plural marriage. Drawing on the life of Joseph Smith, he explained, "There were many truths Joseph Smith could not reveal to the Saints in plainness. Their minds were not prepared to receive them."[48] Further drawing on the history of

The Order Pertaining to the Ancient of Days

the practice, Musser found ways to demonstrate how the manifesto never intended to end the practice for everyone, just as the institution of polygamy in the early Church never initiated the practice for everyone. Within this framework, the Church was not responsible for many practices considered part of the "higher law"—they never were. The Priesthood Council members were responsible for maintaining and promulgating higher laws, such as polygamy and consecration.

Containing the Power of God

Joseph Musser's work on the priesthood is the backbone of current fundamentalist belief and practice, and why many modern fundamentalists place themselves within Mormon history. Polygamous Mormons were excommunicated throughout the 1920s and 1930s but retained a Mormon identity through their continued relationship with priesthood history and reimagined historical narratives that justified the perpetuation of the practice. Musser's writings ultimately argued that there is a priesthood higher than the Church and that the power of God functions independently of earthly institutions, including in the lives of the excommunicated. His priesthood theology did not make the Church unnecessary; it was essential and something the men of the movement believed mattered. It just mattered to a lesser degree than the priesthood:

> We accept the Church of Jesus Christ of Latter-day Saints, as organized, as the propaganda division of the Priesthood, or of God, having as a sacred trust the "proclaiming of the 'Gospel of the Kingdom' to mankind—of guarding and administering God's Holy ordinances necessary to the salvation and exaltation of man." The Church, though out of order, has not been rejected, nor will it be. The Prophet once said: "So long as there are a few people in the Church who are living the fullness of the Gospel, including the Patriarchal order of marriage, God will acknowledge His Church." At the same time, said Joseph Smith, "God will not acknowledge that which he has not called, ordained and chosen." We believe this. We want the Church to grow in strength and power, to be "clear as the moon, and fair as the sun, and terrible as an army with banners"; but in order to reach this glorious position it must first be purged of its false teachings—its fear of men—and with courage and resolution return to the fullness of the Gospel as restored to earth in this dispensation.[49]

This position was not only the foundation for his theological perspectives but also justified his existence as a polygamist man in the twentieth century.

The priesthood writings of Musser were empowering for the excommunicated. They elevated Musser and his coreligionists above the institution and reframed their persecution as a sign of divine providence. As the Church became hostile to polygamous Mormons and more widely spoke against the practice, Musser became increasingly disenfranchised with the Church and further entrenched in his argument that the Church and the priesthood held separate functions. Wilford Woodruff's Manifesto, and Joseph F. Smith's Second Manifesto, were statements by the president of the Church, not the president of the priesthood. For this reason, neither held the authority to end patriarchal marriage. Musser hoped for a day, however, when the leadership of the Church and priesthood would unite as one: "We have learned that a man may be President of the Church and not President of Priesthood, and not even a Prophet; that when the Church is set in order the President of Priesthood will be the President of the Church," he wrote about the manifesto.[50] But, as Church statements became increasingly prevalent, Musser's hostility ultimately led him to question whether the men in the LDS Church had any share in the priesthood.[51]

"Possibly the greatest significance of the 1886 revelation stems not from what it says, but from the reaction of some Church leaders to its existence," wrote Brian Hales of the significance of the revelation that set the precedent for continuing polygamy.[52] He continued, "In the 1920s and 1930s, it was allegedly referred to as a 'scrap of paper' and a 'pretended revelation,' with suggestions that it didn't even exist. In response, Mormon fundamentalists rallied in opposition to what they perceived as a cover up."[53] This remains the case as historians continue to parse out the history of the Mormon fundamentalist movement. As they do, two noteworthy controversies surround the fundamentalist claim to a priesthood outside the Church. The first is the dating of the Woolley account that alleged 1886 ordinations. To date, there is no contemporaneous evidence of ordinations in the Centerville home at the hand of John Taylor. It was not until thirty-six years after the supposed event that the first reference to an ordination circulated in fundamentalist meetings. Another frequently mentioned controversy is the lack of evidence for a Council of Friends in either Mormon scripture or history prior to Musser's 1934 exposition. As Brian Hales explained in his work on the early fundamentalist movement, the supposed ordinations do not align with the Mormon procedure for ordination—"secret ordinations violate an important point of Church procedure established by revelation."[54] These contrary arguments are the current apologetic response to the fundamentalist priesthood claim. Despite such objections, Musser successfully harnessed the history of the Church to lay the foundation for his belief. And on that basis, Musser sought to argue for the persistence of the priesthood's highest principle, plural marriage.

In his work on spiritual power and liturgy, Jonathan Stapley wrote of the disruptive force of the divine that Mormonism harnessed through the formation of religious institutions and hierarchies. "This shattering of heaven's silence was cacophonous," says Stapley, "and Joseph Smith sought to harmonize the outpouring of God's power ecclesiastically in the revelation of priesthood bureaucracy."[55] Even after the Church was established and men were assigned formal priesthood offices, centralization became necessary to ensure control over correct LDS doctrine and practice. Never was centralization more necessary than after the Second Manifesto, when Church leadership confronted growing dissent among members who sought to justify continuing polygamy with history and speculative theology. The Priesthood Correlation Program was among the many centralizing solutions.

The first iteration of a correlation effort began under Joseph F. Smith in 1908 with the organization of a committee chaired by David O. McKay that sought to "strengthen the hierarchical line of authority" within the institutional Church, a mission that mirrored the Progressive Era's own institutionalizing goals.[56] Tangibly, the systematization of priesthood organizations began in 1913 with the formation of auxiliaries and the early formation of teaching manuals.[57] While later correlation programs in the Church reinforced the hierarchy of the institution and emphasized doctrinal standardization, bringing an end to the speculative theology that shaped the nineteenth century, early efforts went largely unnoticed by the average member of the Church. Institutional attempts at standardization did not make their way to the pews, leaving men like Musser justified in their ability to make use of Mormonism in ways that advantaged his revisionist history. Without the centralized doctrines or authority that became associated with Mormonism in the late twentieth century, Musser was free to create his own.

CHAPTER THREE

An Eternal Requirement

The law of plural marriage is the marriage law of the
Priesthood and the only law recognized in the celestial
heavens. Obedience to this law is enjoined on every adult
Latter-day Saint who has the capacity to enter it.
—Saint Joseph White Musser, "The Priesthood's
Supremacy," *Truth* Magazine, July 1936

The New and Everlasting Covenant

"To whom it may concern: At a meeting of the Presidency and the High
Council of the Granite stake of Zion, Joseph W. Musser, after due hearing
and consideration, was excommunicated from the Church of Jesus Christ
of Latter-day Saints for insubordination and disobedience to Church rules
and regulations."[1] This notice, which appeared in the *Deseret News* and as
a newspaper clipping in Musser's diaries, notified Latter-day Saints across
Utah that Joseph Musser was cast out of the Church. For those familiar
with Musser, the reason was well known; he continued to practice and
promote plural marriage after 1904. Prior to the announcement, Musser
underwent two disciplinary hearings. The first, in the Salt Lake City Temple
before the Quorum of the Twelve Apostles in 1909, did not result in formal
discipline. On March 12, 1921, however, he went before the High Council
and faced accusations of living contrary to the Woodruff Manifesto and
marrying a fourth wife.

The accusations of a fourth marriage were dubious; even Musser denied
the allegations. Even though the alleged fourth sealing never happened, he

was *willing* to marry again and retained a belief in the necessity of plural marriage. Despite two announcements from the Church that condemned the practice, he argued that polygamy was the eternal marriage system of the Latter-day Saints and a central part of Mormon cosmology. In his overview of a 1937 General Conference, he lamented that the leadership of the LDS Church was unable to proclaim it boldly:

> I am a polygamist. Celestial or plural marriage is an institution of heaven; it is an eternal law which the Gods themselves have subscribed to, and without strict adherence to which NO MAN receives the highest exaltation in the Celestial heavens. The law has been restored to the worthy among the Saints in this dispensation, never again to be taken from the earth. This nation . . . and all the so called Christian nations of the world, are under condemnation for rejecting God's law of marriage and for aiding in persecuting the Saints for their adherence to it.[2]

The inability for Heber J. Grant to say these words over the pulpit was the evidence Musser needed to argue that the Church had lost its authority. Polygamy was an irrevocable divine mandate and an eternal requirement for anyone claiming a connection to the priesthood.

Like all men in the fundamentalist movement, Musser's view of marriage stemmed from the Restorationist vision of Joseph Smith that sought to restore the Abrahamic covenant and the 1886 Revelation given to John Taylor to ensure the continuation of the practice. Offering an overview of its theological centrality, he explained thus:

> We hold that a companion law to the United Order, is the law of Patri-archal marriage, a necessary element of which is known as plural marriage—the law comprehending the eternity of the marriage revelation; that this law of marriage was restored to earth through the Prophet Joseph Smith, and that its exactments are eternal—the only marriage law recognized as legal in the Celestial heavens, it being the law which our Father in Heaven and His Son Jesus Christ are adhering to. This is the great social law of heaven, through which eternal increase is awarded—the law that makes it possible for men to become Kings and Priests unto the Most High and heirs with Him to all eternity.[3]

Unlike other temporal marriage structures, plural marriage is the foundation of the heavens and the marriage system entertained by all the gods for all eternity. It was the marriage system of the Old Testament patriarchs, the prophet of the last dispensation, and a necessity for God's power to operate on the earth. The end of polygamy was no less than the beginning of apostasy.

All twentieth-century polygamous Mormons believed in the theological significance of plural marriage and sought to retain it contrary to the LDS Church's disavowal. Musser's apologetics were unique for two foundational reasons. During his lifetime, he was among the first to parse the difference between doctrine and policy by publicly proclaiming that the LDS Church's end to polygamy was a political gesture to appease an increasingly hostile US government. That is, the manifesto was merely a policy, not a matter of divine revelation. He followed this differentiation with the argument that polygamy was sociologically beneficial, specifically from the perspective of women. These arguments came together to form Musser's persuasive writing that spoke to individuals who became disassociated from the Church at a precarious time in its history. Musser's writings on plural marriage remain among the most widely distributed pamphlets among those who see themselves in constant confrontation with both LDS Mormons and the legal system that condemns their marriages.

The Mormon Marriage System

Mormons were not the first to practice polygamy in the United States. Nonmonogamy was common among indigenous communities, in colonial New Spain, and throughout the eighteenth-century colonial United States. Within these contexts, polygamy was a way to forge political alliances, acquire resources, and create kinship bonds. Detractors of the Mormon marriage system decried the practice as a "twin relic of barbarism," but polygamy was not uncommon.[4] The practical reasons for Mormon polygamy reflected many of the social reasons for polygamy among other communities. Unlike the rest of polygamous America, however, the Mormon marital system became intimately connected to visions of heaven and deity. Musser separated the Mormon marriage system from other polygamous unions in the nation. He went as far as to declare over the pulpit, "When you come from the old country and say to the government, 'I do not believe in polygamy,' it is true. I and you believe in celestial marriage."[5] He further explained thus:

> World polygamy as defined by the dictionary, is the "mating with more than one of the opposite sex"; the "condition of having more than one

wife or husband at once." Polygamy as a general practice in the so-called Christian world, leads to clandestine associations of the sexes, often resulting in gross immoralities, while "Mormon" polygamy or Celestial marriage, pertains to the Celestial sphere in which God dwells, and is practiced only under direct authority from heaven and according to strictest rules of chastity; "for," said the Lord to Joseph Smith, "they (wives) are given unto him (the husband) to multiply and replenish the earth, according to my commandment, and to fulfill the promise which was given by my Father before the foundation of the world; and for their exaltation in the eternal worlds, that they may bear the souls of men; for herein is the work of my Father continued, that he may be glorified."[6]

From the outset, Musser ensured that polygamy was not separate from the spiritual lives of the Latter-day Saints. It was unlike any earthly marriage system because it was initiated in the eternities.

The date of the plural marriage revelation is contested, with the earliest LDS accounts dating the revival of plural marriage to 1831, when Joseph Smith began studying the Old Testament and read about the polygamous patriarchs. In Musser's account of the revelation, Smith could not reconcile polygamy in the Old Testament with the Book of Mormon's prohibition on the practice in the book of Jacob. The prayers that stemmed from this dilemma were the catalyst for Smith receiving the revelation of "the only order of marriage—celestial or plural—that will enable 'seed to be raised up' unto the Lord: The order of marriage that Abraham and other patriarchs had entered into."[7] For this reason, plural marriage became synonymous with "patriarchal marriage," or "the kind of marriage entered into anciently by such Patriarchs as Abraham, Isaac, Jacob, Moses, and others, and has references to plurality of wives."[8]

Through revelation, Smith received insight that, while monogamy is the rule, God authorized the practice of polygamy at certain times and for specific purposes. Like the polygamous leaders of old, Smith was called to reintroduce the practice as part of the restoration of all things:[9]

Joseph Smith taught that the union between husband and wife may have an eternal existence; that the fruits of that union may continue on; this was all contrary to the sectarian notion that the marriage covenant lasts only "unto death do you part." It is through this eternal union that men are permitted to become Lord of lords, King of kings, and Gods in the eternities, their wives and children following and assisting them in the building up of their kingdom. Also that Celestial Marriage embraces, as a necessary element thereof, Plural marriage—the "Law of Abraham."[10]

Several years after Smith received the revelation to reinstitute plural marriage, the first documented plural marriage in this dispensation occurred on April 5, 1841, with the sealing of Louisa Beaman to Joseph Smith on the bank of the Mississippi River in Nauvoo, Illinois. Beaman and Smith's other close associates, who entered into plural marriages early in the practice's history, pledged to keep the new marriage system private. Marriage was a Mormon ordinance accessible to all people, but the "full consummation" of celestial marriage was reserved for a select few.[11] Musser was among the first, in closing his book introducing polygamy, to name the plural wives of Joseph Smith.

It was not until more than a decade later, on July 12, 1843, that Smith recorded what became Doctrine and Covenants 132, colloquially referred to as the plural marriage revelation. The revelation became one of the most controversial documents in Latter-day Saint history, with a lasting impact on Mormon doctrine and practice. With the revelation, Mormon marriages were reimagined as part of an "expanding network of interconnected familial sealings with dynastic overtones."[12] From the earliest iterations of the revelation, the eternal family structure and plural marriage were inextricably linked: "A BELIEF in the eternity of the marriage covenant renders a belief in plural marriage inescapable. The two are inseparably connected. In this belief plural marriage is not merely a permitted indulgence for the term of mortality, but an eternal requirement."[13]

Closely tied to the familial aspects of the revelation was the "language of deification," which linked the practice to exaltation.[14] In the nineteenth-century Mormon context, the families forged on altars were "the lingua franca of an exaltation that was steeply gendered and rooted in polygamy."[15] Exaltation required plural unions. "Plural marriage and not monogamy is the order of heaven: and therefore, in order to get into heaven—that heaven in which our Father and Mother reside and to become 'joint heirs' with them, the order of 'plural marriage must obtain.'"[16] Through polygamy, Latter-day Saints were equipped to multiply and replenish the earth, participate in the first resurrection, and eternally propagate worlds.[17] The command for Abraham to practice plural marriage implied that human beings were incapable of doing these things without polygamy.

The necessity of plural marriage, once reserved for chosen members of the faith, was first expanded under the leadership of Brigham Young, who preached the necessity of the practice. In 1866, Brigham Young famously preached, "The only men who become Gods, even the sons of God, are those who enter into polygamy."[18] For Young and his fundamentalist successors, human exaltation was intimately tied to plural marriage as the "only law recognized in the celestial heavens."[19] Drawing on quotes from Brigham Young, Joseph F. Smith, Wilford Woodruff, William Clayton, and others, Musser argued that "eternal laws have eternal applications."[20] Even before his entry into fundamentalism, the importance of polygamy as the marital structure of exalted men was part of Musser's theology. In diary entries after the 1890 Manifesto, he recounted learning in stake meetings about Jesus's polygamous unions:

> I attended a reception tendered [by] the Patriarchs of the Stake at Prest. Smart's home, by himself. . . . Apostle Teasdale arose to speak briefly, and was led to speak on the principle of patriarchal and plural marriage. He stated no patriarch in the church could be such unless he believed this principle. Scoffed the idea that Jesus Christ was not a married man, and taught that he was not only married, but had more than one wife. He had all the experience that we are supposed to get. Said that only wicked people opposed the principle.[21]

In line with the overarching claim of the fundamentalist movement, Musser was not culivating new doctrines and practices. He was reinstating the historic position of the Church, that polygamy was a necessity and not a matter of preference.

From the beginning, the problem was the national government. The United States and neighbors of Latter-day Saints throughout the Church's history did not accept the Mormon marriage system and its theological justification. In the earliest years of the faith, polygamy made Mormons irreligious in the eyes of the nation.[22] For this reason, the purported end to plural marriage in 1890 and 1904 were controversial to Mormons who wanted to retain the practice. For them, the policy to end plural marriage indicated that Mormonism was aligning with modernity. Musser, for example, commented, "The policy of the Church to popularize itself with the world has forced upon it the adoption of many sectarian ideas that are causing 'dry rot' among the rank and file of its members."[23] Musser hoped for a Church that held fast to its peculiarity in the face of modernization. Such was not the case for institutional Mormonism.

Musser's resistance to modernity was not unique. His reaction to doctrine and institutional authority growing more centralized—but also more secular—was typical of movements within religious institutions that "modernized" in unsatisfactory ways. Historically, divisions and schisms in Roman Catholicism were located in the search for an authentic expression of the faith in reaction to modernizations deemed incompatible with its mission of preserving a historical Christianity to the end of the age. The most apparent example was in the wake of the Second Vatical Council, the 21st ecumenical council of the Roman Catholic Church that met between 1962 and 1965 with the goal of updating the church to meet the needs of the twentieth century. The very purpose of the council, an *aggiornamiento* or update, caused concern for Catholics who joined a traditionalist movement that sought to preserve a particular kind of Catholicism associated with the 1570 Roman Missal and an attachment to the form of the Mass developed at the sixteenth-century Council of Trent.[24]

Celestial Marriage

Testimonials by early Church leaders shaped Musser's perspective on plural marriage and its continued centrality after the First and Second Manifestos. Editorials and public commentary were central to his advocacy, but it was his pamphlets that served as a platform for "extensive testimonials from Apostles, Prophets and other holy men and women of God," a compilation of statements that supported the fundamentalist position.[25] In addition to men and women with whom Latter-day Saints were familiar, Musser incorporated testimonials and perspectives from outside the faith, citing the early Christian Church Fathers and governmental officials on issues of freedom of conscience and the nature of God. This tactic allowed Musser to frame his perspective as one of logical continuity and as representative of an authentic expression of Mormonism, in contrast to the spirit of apostasy that led to changes in the institutional LDS Church.[26] Fundamentalism was not a reaction, in Musser's view. It was the only Mormonism true to its founder's vision.

Musser emphasized polygamy as the marital system of the celestial sphere, the highest degree of Mormon heavenly cosmology. While the use of *celestial* as synonymous with plural marriage was not controversial during the time of his marriages, it increasingly became a way that the fundamentalist movement separated itself from the LDS Church. During the twentieth century, the LDS Church reimagined celestial marriage as synonymous with the doctrine of the eternal monogamous family.[27] In contrast, Musser retained the nineteenth-century definition that required polygamy:

> The word "Celestial," from the latin "Caelum," implies in the sense we use the term, sky or heaven—the place where God has His seat of power. Celestial marriage lasts not only during mortal life but continues in the post-mortal existence and throughout the eternities. Celestial glory, then has reference to the glory that perfected beings enjoy—the glory that obtains where God is, who, of course, enjoys the highest exaltation in that glory. A tradition has grown among the Latter-day Saints that Celestial marriage may be comprehended either in the monogamous or patriarchal form, when the ceremony is performed.[28]

The Latter-day Saint doctrine of eternal families is based on the same revelation that revived the practice of polygamy. The Mormon temple sealing, which retains polygamous language, similarly draws on the revelation. The lasting ways that polygamy informs Mormon marriage led Musser to believe that the connection between plural marriage and eternal marriage was obvious: "From the foregoing array of testimony relative to the true meaning of the law of Celestial Marriage, surely no sober minded Latter-day Saint will be so simple as to regard a monogamous union, by whomsoever it may be consummated, a fulfillment of the law as it was received and established through the Prophet Joseph Smith."[29]

Musser did not intend to denigrate monogamous marriage. As plural marriage was an eternal requirement for families to continue in the afterlife, he believed that all marriage pointed toward polygamy:

> The marriage of one wife to a husband in the Celestial order, as explained by President Smith is only the beginning of the law of celestial marriage, the full consummation thereof being accomplished in the plural act and its proper abidance. The taking of one wife, as the act relates to the law of celestial marriage, may be likened to an alien filing his first papers—a "declaration of intention" to become a citizen of the United States. Stopping there, however, he never becomes a citizen; there are

other preparations and papers necessary; and so in entering into Celestial marriage other steps are necessary.[30]

By Musser's fourth plural sealing, polygamy was no longer the exception reserved for the select few, as in Smith's day. Plural marriage was an eternal law in the lives of the Saints, and the willingness to accept polygamy determined the eternality of marriages.

The celestial nature of polygamy was best exemplified in the frequent discussion of the gods and their wives. In priesthood meetings and sacrament talks, the leaders of the fundamentalist movement pointed to Adam's and Jesus's exaltation and the wives who accompanied Them into the heavens. Woolley, for example, posited Martha, Mary, Phoebe, Sarah, Rebecca, Josephine, and Mary Magdalene as the wives of Jesus.[31] In Woolley's account, the number mattered. "To be the head of a dispensation, seven wives necessary. Five wives necessary in the holding of the Keys to the Kingdom or of the Church or to the Patriarchal Order."[32] The speculative theology in the movement's early years concretized the reality that eternal, celestial, and plural marriage were three names for the same eternal social structure.

Revelation or Policy

In 1862, the United States passed legislation that sought to end the practice of polygamy in the Utah Territory. The nation's concern over polygamy placed the Latter-day Saints in a difficult position, requiring a choice between citizenship and God's commandment for marriage. Latter-day Saints chose the latter and continued the practice despite an escalation in legal enforcement. Part of the escalation was passage of the federal Edmunds Act in 1882, increasing the penalty for the practice to a six-month prison sentence and a $300 fine. In 1887, the stakes intensified again with the Edmunds-Tucker Act, which placed the Church in jeopardy of disincorporation and seizure of its property, including its temples. For people who believed in the saving ordinances of the Church, the loss of temples endangered the foundations of the faith. Growing LDS concern led President Wilford Woodruff to pray for answers to the plight of the faithful. On September 25, 1890, Woodruff recorded that he was "under the necessity of acting for the Temporal Salvation of the Church."[33] That day, the Church issued Official Declaration 1,

62

an official announcement on the Church's marital practice. The document explained, "We are not teaching polygamy, or plural marriage, nor permitting any person to enter into its practice."[34]

The language of the First Manifesto sought to remove speculation over whether the Latter-day Saints were practicing an unlawful marital system. The point was not lost on Musser and his coreligionists, who felt the LDS Church was in error. Although the Church leadership sustained the manifesto, leadership was not unified on the matter. John W. Taylor and John Henry Smith expressed hesitancy about the document, resulting in years of tension made visible by the postmanifesto plural sealings at the hands of Apostles who questioned the end of the practice. During the October 1890 General Conference, the document that became the manifesto was presented to the Church for a sustaining vote and later added to the Doctrine and Covenants. The vote to sustain the document was unanimous among Church members but several abstained themselves. Those who abstained raised questions about the practical implementation of the document, namely the status of already sealed plural families. Among the abstainers was Joseph W. Musser, who, in fact, married additional wives after the manifesto entered the Doctrine and Covenants.

Musser was among the first to question the nature of the manifesto publicly, suggesting that Woodruff's statement was a matter of policy, not a change in the core doctrine of the faith. His first speculation that the manifesto was a political maneuver by Church leadership came in 1935, in an appropriately titled *Truth* editorial, "Was the Manifesto a Revelation?"[35] At the time of the editorial, *Truth* had been in circulation for only one month with the stated mission of outlining the "fundamentals that govern existence."[36] The editorial responded to an 1891 defense of the manifesto in the *Deseret News*. Musser's primary argument was that the manifesto did not open with "Thus saith the Lord," implying the words of God, a common critique of policy changes:

> But all the childish babble and prattle about the Manifesto being a revelation from God and putting an end to the practice of the Patriarchal order of marriage (except as it affects the Church as an organized institution) is pure buncombe; and one understanding the situation may be pardoned for feeling indignant when the present leading brethren who were fully conversant with the facts at that time, continue to insist on camouflaging the situation and attaching reproach to many honorable men and

women, with their offspring, who have been led to obey the command of God with reference to the marriage covenant."[37]

Musser's conclusion, and that of others, was that the manifesto was a response to people's demands, not God's will.

"It is just as clear, too, that the Manifesto was never intended to stop the practice of plural marriage, for the practice went on," Musser argued in his defense of continuing the practice. That the manifesto did not put an official end to the practice, coupled with the fact that leadership approved numerous marriages after the 1890 Manifesto, led many to question whether the manifesto was a temporary suspension of polygamy rather than a conclusive end.[38] Musser extensively documented postmanifesto marriages as a compelling case for the former. Of course, Musser's knowledge was not only secondhand; he was among the men who married under Church authority after the Woodruff Manifesto. Representative of his historical examples was Abraham H. Cannon, who "entered into the principle some time after the Manifesto was adopted as a law of the Church" with his marriage to Lilian Hamlin.[39] Extrapolating from this example, Musser concluded that it was likely "Hundreds entered the practice. Arrangements were made for the rites to be performed in Canada and Mexico."[40]

Musser's claim that hundreds entered into polygamous marriages after the manifesto, including leaders, became a point of contention between the fundamentalist movement and the leaders of the LDS Church. Heber J. Grant, the president of the LDS Church at the time of Musser's writing, fixated particularly on the claim that leaders in the LDS Church were polygamous or solemnizing plural marriages. In the 1933 statement at General Conference that became colloquially known as the Third Manifesto, the subject came to the forefront. Grant highlighted the concern that polygamous Mormons were "maligning the leaders of the Church" and were leveling accusations that were both damaging reputations and causing public embarrassment.[41] Grant's comments on polygamy are indicative of the way that the fundamentalist movement, particularly its position on polygamy, was never wholly absent from the mind of institutional leadership. While Musser's pamphlets on polygamy likely did not circulate to the extent he claimed, in Sunday schools across the intermountain West, they circulated enough to cause concern among Church leaders.

The theological necessity of polygamy, as espoused by early leaders of the LDS Church, led Musser to conclude that the end of Church-sanctioned plural marriages was politically expedient and based on motivations outside revelation. In his mind, the end to polygamy was an impossibility:

> In closing, let us again emphasize the fact that the issuance of the Manifesto came in response to the demands of the people; President Woodruff signed it under a permissive grant. That he did not subscribe to it in spirit was well known by his intimates at the time. He did what he said he "felt inspired" to do; he doubtless did the best he knew how under the circumstances.[42]

The framing of the manifesto as a concession began the long-standing tradition of Mormon fundamentalism's articulation of itself as a more authentic form of Mormonism that was willing to retain the more difficult principles of the Restoration in the face of adversity. Rather than succumb to what Peter Coviello refers to as the "disciplinary efforts" of governmental intervention, Musser reimagined the Church as an institution that sought to remain faithful to its founding principles, rather than comport itself in harmony with American ideals.[43]

Robbed of Its Glory

Musser's assertion that the Church bowed to governmental pressure when it renounced polygamy was well received by his readers and remained the central argument against the First and Second Manifestos. While his objections in *Truth* remained his most significant contribution to the history of Mormon polygamy, one of his more unique arguments for polygamy's continuation was his appeal to womanhood and sexuality in advocating the practice. Not to be confused as an early advocate for women's liberation, Musser was one of the few leaders in the fundamentalist movement who spoke directly about the women of his community and their marital choice and reproductive health. Women's lives did not hang in the background but were brought to the forefront as a justification for the controversial marital practice.

Central to his arguments for women's involvement in plural marriage was the practice's connection to exaltation. The doctrine of exaltation depended on the entire human family, including women. Like Mormon men, who recognized themselves as following in the footsteps of Adam through their mortality and polygamous marriages, women foresaw their future exalted state as one of deity. To demonstrate the point, Musser frequently quotes women, most notably Eliza R. Snow's poetry, which centered on the polygamous life of Eve:

> Obedience will the same bright garland weave,
> As it has done for your great Mother, Eve,
> For all her daughters on the earth, who will
> All my requirements sacredly fulfill.
> And what to Eve, though in her mortal life,
> She'd been the first, the tenth, or fiftieth wife?
> What did *she care*, when in her lowest state,
> Whether by fools, consider'd small, or great?
> 'Twas all the same with her—she prov'd her worth—
> She's now the Goddess and the Queen of Earth.[44]

Within Musser's theological framework, women's exaltation was connected to their status as wives and mothers. Early Church leaders who centered polygamy in their theology of godhood, such as Brigham Young, supported this argument.

Eternal polygamous unions awaited the exalted. From 1932 on, Joseph Musser recorded accounts from the Woolley School of the Prophets that explicitly mentioned women in the role of deity. In a talk given to members of his Priesthood Council on March 6, Lorin C. Woolley offered names for the wives of Adam, making them the goddesses of this world:

Adam probably had three wives on earth before Mary, Mother of Jesus.

Eve—meaning	1st	
Phoebe "	2nd	
Sarah "	3rd, probably mother of Seth. Joseph of Armenia [Arimathea], proxy husband of Mary had one wife before Mary and four additional after.[45]	

In addition to the wives of Adam, Woolley further speculated that the wives of Jesus were "Martha (Industry), Mary (of god), Phoebe, Sarah (Sacrifice), Rebecca (given of God), Josephine (Daughter of Joseph), Mary Magdalen, and Mary, Martha's sister."[46] Woolley's comment did not include context or additional insight, but his statements initiated a tradition of naming the women deified through polygamous relationships. In this theology, women were visible. The theology of naming the wives of gods gave women the necessary language to make their eternal future a tangible reality.

Six years after Woolley's first reference to exalted women, Musser expanded the doctrine to increase the mentioning of women in the creation narrative. In his 1938 Mother's Day editorial, he drew on Eliza R. Snow's poetry to comment on the "great and glorious truths pertaining to women's true position in the creations of the Gods" in her poems.[47] He wrote, "A Goddess came down from her mansions of glory to bring the spirits of her children down after her, in their myriads of branches and their hundreds of generations!"[48] "The celestial Masonry of Womanhood! The other half of the grand patriarchal economy of heavens and earth!" he declared of the elevated state his cosmology supposedly afforded women in plural unions.[49] Women were part of the polygamous cosmological structure powered by the priesthood. According to his theology, the birthing of the cosmological order necessitated womanhood and a matriarchal power that worked alongside the patriarchal priesthood. Before the temporal existence of this earth's god, womanhood manifested in the eternal structure of the "Trinity of Mothers—Eve the Mother of the world; Sarah the Mother of the covenant; Zion the Mother of celestial sons and daughters—the Mother of the new creation of Messiah's reign, which shall give to earth the crown of her glory and the cup of joy after all her ages of travail."[50]

In response to his 1909 meeting with Church leaders, Musser wrote, "I believe God intended that every woman should have the opportunity of becoming a mother, and if her soul desired to, the means would be justified. Since the Church therefore has thru the statement of a man, not pretended to be a revelation, discontinued the obligation of its members to practice the principle, it now remains for each individual to follow his personal conviction in the matter."[51] Among the individuals who followed their convictions were the many women who either joined the fundamentalist movement with their husbands or converted on their own. Musser's writing about women was not without problems, perpetuating a pedestalization of Mormon women. Nevertheless, his work afforded them agency to make decisions about their marriages and families.

Musser presented the end of LDS polygamy as an event that disproportionately affected women. Like others at the time, Musser viewed women as inherently more religious than men, making polygamy a necessity. Without it, the eternal state of women was at stake and "heaven would be robbed of its glory, men and women must go on in singleness devoid of all hope of eternal progress."[52] Musser was not the first to argue a women's case for polygamy or argue that polygamy was the system by which "Men were lionized and women exalted."[53] Long before the fundamentalist movement, women argued in favor of the polygamous marital system as beneficial for all involved. Arguments were often based on child spacing and concern about moral failures, namely prostitution. Most notably, Belinda Marden Pratt, the sixth wife of Apostle Parley Pratt, who remarried Musser's father, became an apologist for plural marriage and emphasized the agency of Abraham's wife, who instituted the practice.[54]

Musser's concern about marital choice was not in the abstract. Many women in the Mormon fundamentalist movement desired plural marriage and, by extension, an assurance of their exaltation. During the 1930s and 1940s, Mormon women faced governmental prosecution for choosing to practice polygamy. When Musser wrote of these women, he presented them as persecuted simply for "seeking honorable motherhood."[55] A notable example was the excommunication of Charles Zitting's plural wife, Elvera C. Olson Zitting. After the announcement of her 1928 excommunication in the Deseret News, Musser transformed her story into an account of a woman who simply sought the promises of her faith.[56] LDS Church leaders, specifically President Heber J. Grant, supported government intervention saying, "Such action might put a stop to the teachings of people who are today destroying the virtue of good women who are silly enough to listen to them."[57] The reality is that the women of the fundamentalist movement were anything but "silly." Many recognized the potential advantages of membership in the movement. Musser's own fourth wife, Lucy O. Kmetzsch, found her place within the movement shortly after her excommunication from the LDS Church in 1934. Her and her sisters all married prominent members of the fundamentalist movement, including Goldie Kmetzsch's marriage to Lorin C. Woolley and Anna Kmetzsch's marriage to J. Leslie Broadbent.

In addition to marital choice, Musser articulated the societal benefits of polygamy that he viewed as more helpful to women. According to Musser, "Polygamy, as practiced by the Saints, makes for better men and women, while monogamy, as lived today, tends in the opposite direction. Polygamy, under strict supervision, is the social law of heaven, while monogamy, instituted as it was as a purely Gentile and Pagan rite, is the social law of Lucifer."[58] Polygamy was beneficial to society, specifically in sexual regulation, something Belinda Pratt also argued in her defense of the practice. Like later polygamists, she lauded polygamy for its ability to lead to "the chastity of women, and to sound health and morals in the constitution of their children."[59] Musser identified polygamous marriages as the ideal marital relationship for raising children, and the purity of the marriages was paramount for the children's spiritual well-being. In his recordings of Woolley's revelations, Musser noted, "That there are great and mighty spirits waiting to come forth when the channel is sufficiently pure to welcome them is sure, [sic] but they cannot be born under conditions of lust."[60] Like Pratt, women who followed Musser's teachings were inspired by his words on sexuality. Rulon Allred's half-sister, Rhea Allred Kunz, and fellow polygamist, Jenna Vee Hammon became advocates for the marital law that Musser promoted. Kunz's support focused on the "self-control" in marriage and her conviction that sexuality in plural marriage would not transform into lust, the "devil's counterfeit."[61]

Musser did not offer much explanation for the practice, except that the law of purity within plural marriage benefited women's reproductive health. Musser first encountered the principles that became the law of purity from his leader, Lorin C. Woolley, who taught "Purity of Celestial Marriage" as a divine commandment and requirement for plural marriage.[62] According to Woolley, laws that regulated sexuality were the only way the Saints could "bring on the Millennium" and participate in the "Celestial population" of the Millennium.[63] Of the men who followed Woolley, only Musser and J. Leslie Broadbent believed its significance, Musser being most closely associated with the codification of the higher law of chastity after Woolley's death:[64]

> The Lord showed me, through the Spirit, further light pertaining to Celestial Marriage, that when the Saints live the fullness of that law, there will be no sexual intercourse or sexual indulgences, except for the purpose of bringing children into mortality. Men will respect the wishes of their wives and never approach them except when invited, and women will never invite their husbands except to have children; and during pregnancy there will be no sexual relations.[65]

One of the most central aspects of the law of purity was the prohibition of birth control, a societal trend that concerned Musser, who taught the importance of polygamy as the avenue to "raise of seed."[66] In his writing on Short Creek, he noted the lack of birth control and its connection to virtuous womanhood:

> No one, however corrupt he personally may be, after living among these Short Creek people, even if it should be discovered that one or two of them do have more wives than one, will say that they are immoral. Short Creek wives do not engage in the practice of "birth control," nor do their husbands object to additional children being born and added to their burdens. They are virtuous women; modesty is written in their countenances; they laugh with an honest ring while their eyes sparkle with lustrous beauty; they shun the vice of prudery and deal in frankness.[67]

Musser's depiction of an idyllic polygamous society was juxtaposed against a worldly image. In his account of worldliness, Musser revives nineteenth-century race science that argued for correct sexuality as the basis of family and societal health:

> There are no harlots at Short Creek and no childless wives, except as nature may have appointed. Children come into life there clear-eyed, strong, healthy and promising; no sexual diseases dwarf or shorten their lives. Short Creek has no doctors or drug store; lip stick and rouge are not needed, nature has given the girls a more comely endowment. For the most part women, properly trained, look after their sisters in childbirth. These wives look forward to maternal increase with a peace of mind and joy that "race suicide" and "birth control" advocates may never know. They are attached to their husbands by bonds of purest love, and they in turn enjoy the love and protective care of their husbands, who are true to them, clean and honorable. It cannot be truthfully said of any of these husbands, that they ever wronged a woman.[68]

Although Musser lauded Short Creek for its support of women, the reality he described was not long-lived in the towns on the Arizona Strip. More and more often, Musser became aware of the harm many women experienced at the hands of "placement marriage," the practice of arranged marriage under the direction of priesthood leaders. Placement marriage had not always been standard practice within the polygamous community.

In her work on Mormon fundamentalism, Marianne Watson identified placement marriages as a 1940s development that rendered the marriage age for women younger than had previously been known in the movement.[69] Musser's opposition to one such marriage, of the daughter of Joseph Lyman Jessop, was one of the most decisive disagreements in the movement that overturned much of Musser's focus on marital choice. For all Musser's emphasis on women's agency, placement marriage became the standard form of marriage in Short Creek after Musser's death.

CHAPTER FOUR

That the Poor May Be Exalted

Any economic system that makes for dissatisfaction
and misery instead of happiness and peace is
born of the world. God's system, when given full
expression, while wisely providing that man MUST work
for that which he consumes, fixes a proper niche,
socially and economically, for each individual.

—Saint Joseph White Musser,
The Economic Order of Heaven

In July 1933, Diamond Oil Company terminated Musser's eleven-year employment with the company. Prior to the termination, Musser experienced years of financial difficulty. The need to care for a polygamous family exacerbated the problem. On March 5, 1933, Musser recorded the closing of the banks and the need for national repentance. As he explained, "The Lord has withdrawn his Spirit from the people who will not turn to him, and the beginning of a cleaning up has come. Death and misery will stalk the land and this Government will give way for the real Gov't of God. The righteous must stand in holy places, while the wicked are swept from earth. God help me to stand and endure."[1] Musser's financial precarity, coupled with the failing banking system of the United States, catalyzed his fervor to implement a consecration program to ensure the financial stability of the faithful.

Musser was not alone in financial hardship at this time. The Great Depression devastated Utah and caused a 35.9 percent unemployment rate in the state by 1932.[2] By the end of the Depression, almost one-third of the state had received aid from the Reconstruction Finance Corporation.[3] Amid the economic turmoil, the LDS Church established its own social safety nets to aid members hit by the nation's economic collapse. The programs' purpose was religious and political, "From its founding at the height of the Great Depression, Mormon welfare has served an important role in tying Mormonism to American political conservatism. In fact, LDS social policy provided one of the first opportunities for economic and religious conservatives to make their peace with the Mormon faith."[4] As the New Deal rose in popularity, the LDS Church feared the potential impact of social programs on their membership, particularly the concern that some of the faithful would "succumb to a 'dole mentality.'"[5] To forestall that possibility, the Church took the changing political and social climate as an opportunity to create a parallel welfare system.

The Church's welfare program was marketed to the nation as "the better, more American, more constitutional way out of the Depression."[6] But members of the Church did not gravitate away from government assistance. Utah residents differed with their church leaders in their views on government welfare. Most supported Franklin D. Roosevelt's second presidential nomination and New Deal policies, despite their leadership's outspoken opposition to the Democratic candidate.[7] During the Depression, leaders of the Church took the opportunity at the General Conference of the Church of Jesus Christ of Latter-day Saints to warn against debt and encourage self-reliance and preparedness. At this time, Mormonism and political conservativism became deeply intertwined. Economic certainty became the marker of righteous sainthood. Those who struggled during the nation's most significant collapse were placed in a difficult position.

The position in which many excommunicated Latter-day Saints found themselves compounded the already difficult period of the Great Depression. The Great Depression, coupled with the religious persecution that caused some Latter-day Saints to lose their employment and religious community, brought into question the promise of a Zion where there would be "no poor among them."[8] As an excommunicated member of the LDS Church, Musser did not have access to the social programs established by the Church for its members or the community support that many found for themselves in this challenging time. In response, Musser looked to history and found hope in the possibility of reestablishing the United Order, an early Mormon communitarian program based on the law of consecration, the command to dedicate possession and talents to the building of God's

Kingdom. The communitarian vision of early Mormonism transformed the fundamentalist community from a fledgling group of outcasts into a unified body of believers who eventually incorporated aspects of the United Order into their rival organizations. Through Musser's writing, the United Order became yet another aspect of the early Mormon faith that fundamentalists pointed to as a necessity discarded by the dominant movement for the sake of convenience.[9]

The Church and New Deal

In 1933, the United States implemented programs, reforms, and regulations to alleviate the financial challenges that many Americans faced during the Great Depression. In his telling of the state of the US financial system, Musser argued that Americans were witnessing the logical end of participation in worldly financial systems:

> Under the world system frequent financial disruptions have occurred from the beginning of time, a recent one taking place during and following World War I, culminating in the financial collapse in 1929, and resulting in the loss to millions of people in the United States, through banks and other failures, of their life savings, until in March 1933, every bank in the United States was closed by the order of the President.[10]

In Musser's account of contemporary events, the United States was not alone in its struggling finances. He wrote about starvation, global inflation, and homelessness among those who had served in the armed forces. The only solution was to adopt the economics of heaven, which Musser believed were available to all people.

In response to financial distress, the United States inaugurated the New Deal, a program welcomed by many Latter-day Saints, who sought government aid in a time of financial insecurity. Despite widespread support among Church members, the Church leadership grew concerned about Latter-day Saint reliance on secular support. Leaders expressed this concern over the pulpit, warning against government systems that leaders perceived as a blight on the American Church. President Heber J. Grant forcefully stated, "I believe that there is a growing disposition among the people to try to get something from the government of the United States with little hope of ever paying it back. I think this is all wrong."[11] In these statements, at the Church's most widely viewed pulpit, Grant collapsed the divide between the religious and political.

Beginning in the 1920s, the Church established assistance programs for the faithful, most overseen by the Presiding Bishopric and the Relief Society. Implementation of New Deal programs under government agencies, however, financially sidelined charitable and religious organizations, including the Relief Society, and placed further emphasis on governmental support as the primary avenue for financial aid. As Colleen McDannell documented in her work on Mormon women in the twentieth century, movement away from religious aid organizations toward government programs most affected the place of women in the Church hierarchy. In response, the Church's women's organization reorganized into a government program the short-lived District 7 of the Salt Lake County Department of Public Welfare.

The changing economic climate spurred the leaders of the LDS Church to political involvement. J. Reuben Clark attended the Republican National Convention in 1936, and Heber J. Grant expressed hope in an Alfred Landon presidential victory. Political sentiments bled into General Conference talks and emphasized the industrious fervor of the Latter-day Saints. Such developments became a point of questioning for Musser, who viewed the words of Church leaders as hollow in light of struggling Church members:

> The hackneyed cry of "pay your tithing and be blessed" has lost its glamour among a people left by their shepherds to drift and roam in the wilderness, crying for relief and all the time going deeper into bondage. Let the law of consecration, followed by the true law of tithing be inaugurated, and Zion will really begin to flourish, and the lost sheep of Israel will gladly return to their fold.[12]

For those facing economic uncertainty, the Church's emphasis on individual economic self-reliance seemed nothing more than a distant hope. It stood in stark contrast to the communitarian ideals of the nineteenth-century faith.

While still a faithful member of the LDS Church and struggling to care for a growing family, Musser considered the possibility of living the United Order as part of the "law of our temporal salvation" with his stake president, William Smart:[13]

> "United Order": At 9 o'clock my wife and I met with Smart and his family. And we effected an organization of what we hope will be a

Community of Interests or the "United Order." Prest. Smart presided over the Meeting. We came fasting and the occasion was a serious one. He spoke at length about the possibilities in the Patriarchal form of Marriage, going from that to the principle of the "United" Order. His desire for years had been to live this grand principle, that he might receive experience and development and be in a position to serve the Lord with more purpose.[14]

Practically, his early vision to live the United Order with other members of his stake began with placing all property is common and establishing an education center in Provo to instruct people on the mission of the United Order.[15] Throughout his diary entries, Musser's various plans to live the United Order demonstrate that communitarianism was desired among people who struggled to live plural marriage. Many faithful found the Church unhelpful in the matter.

The fundamentalist Mormons viewed the lack of financial solutions during the Depression as especially concerning because of their polygamous faith that promoted large families with many dependents. Considering the Mormon family structure in light of American capitalism, Musser chastised the US economy, arguing that the government succumbed to the logical ends of the world's economic system: "There are two general economic systems in vogue, one based upon the laws of heaven—God's system—the other, a counterfeit. The latter, designated as the world system, was under the direct control of the 'Prince of Darkness.'"[16] Unlike the Church and its faltering economic structure, Musser sought to revive "God's economic system," which, "so far as it has been revealed (and enough has been revealed to arrest the attention of the nations of the world for the present) is clear, definite and understandable. . . . The fruits of the Lord's system are protection, plenty, peace, happiness, expansion, and eternal lives."[17]

Faced with the faults of the American economic system at the height of the depression, the men of the fundamentalist movement were left wondering why the Latter-day Saints stopped living God's economic system. To this question, Musser simply replied that the end of Mormon communitarianism stemmed from the Latter-day Saints being "deeply traditional in the philosophy of the world. Selfishness, the spirit of aggrandizement, greed, competition, were too strongly imbedded in their natures to accept the sacred law in totum."[18] Looking back on the history of the Church, Musser argued that the lack of emphasis on consecration was a primary reason for the hardship Latter-day Saints faced throughout their history and the reason they would fail again in the future:

> The settlement of the Saints in Jackson County, Missouri, was conditioned on obedience to this law, for Zion can be built up on no other principle than adherence to the fulness of the Gospel of which this law was part. The Saints failed. Selfishness and greed overcame them. They forfeited their right to divine protection, hence were driven from their inheritances. . . . After the Prophet's martyrdom and the Saints found sanctuary in the valleys of the Rockies they were again taught the great law. Many Orders were organized, thrived and blossomed forth for a season, then, under the scorching sun of traditional error, the plant withered and dried; and instead of the Saints becoming a mighty people economically, as will be their final destiny, they are now in bondage."[19]

Despite the lack of preparedness to live total consecration, Musser foresaw a time when the entire world, religious and nonreligious alike, would seek the counsel of the polygamous Mormons on the implementation of the United Order to alleviate financial distress. In response to Church leaders who commented on the evils of financial bondage without offering alternatives, Musser admonished:

> It would be well for the leaders of Ephraim to emulate the example of our Short Creek Saints, introduce it among the more humble of the Saints here who are willing to live God's holy laws; cease seeking to destroy those who are courageously and faithfully blazing the way leading to perfect economic existence. Let the Short Creek Saints teach the body of the Church the lesson they are learning in the midst of persecution, and the distress spoken of by Elder Richards and other speakers, will soon disappear.[20]

Offering Short Creek as an example to the LDS Church, Musser again portrayed the polygamous Mormons as more faithful than they to the vision of Joseph Smith. During the nineteenth century, Mormonism's opponents argued that the faith would be unable to withstand modernity. Brigham Young, with his movement West and industrialization, proved them wrong. Mormonism underwent a process of secularization through its adoption of American industry and became an accepted part of the American religious landscape.[21] While celebrated by many of the faithful, the adoption of American economic and political norms was the outcome that Musser feared. Reviving the Law of Heaven was the solution.

A Law of Heaven

In this time of significant change in the nation and Church, the excommunicated were in a more insecure situation than their LDS neighbors. Those whom Heber J. Grant labeled "United Order enthusiasts . . . already cut off [from] the Church," a title Musser recorded in his April 1935 reflections on the LDS General Conference, not only lost their religious community, they lost their ability to participate in the social safety nets the institutional Church offered.[22] With nowhere to turn for financial stability, Musser looked back to the history of the Latter-day Saints for consolation. Mormons were historically accustomed to hardship, both social and financial. Like the polygamists of the 1930s, the early Saints struggled to care for large families when they first settled the Salt Lake Valley. In the wake of poverty and immense need, the historic memory of the early Mormon communitarian initiatives offered an answer. The law was "designed to provide economic salvation for the Saints, 'that the poor shall be exalted, in that the rich are made low' (D&C 104:16) or brought to a level of equality."[23]

The need to ensure economic stability was inseparable from the large family structure that Mormonism fostered through the institution of polygamy. Musser frequently wrote of polygamy and United Order as "the highest rungs in the gospel ladder revealed to man" that, "when they are gained[,] one is literally living the fulness of the Gospel. One is the complement of the other."[24] For this reason, his history of Mormon communitarianism goes back to 1831, the same year Musser gave for the restoration of plural marriage. The Doctrine and Covenants revealed a system whereby God is not a respecter of persons or private property. "He does not dress one in robes and another in rags; does not gut one with bounties and delicacies and assign the other to a life of despair and starvation."[25] In short, Musser took Smith's revelation to heart: "If ye are not one, ye are not mine."[26] Because of the religious nature of his economic ideals and his belief that "with God all things are spiritual," Musser did not see the New Deal as adequately equipped to handle the outcome of the Mormon marital system.[27]

Although New Deal economics was ill-equipped to address the needs of the polygamous Mormons, Musser argued, the priesthood was uniquely situated to provide for the material needs of the Latter-day Saints. In his writing on the division between the priesthood and the Church, he outlined a theoretical model for a priesthood-operated government and social welfare structure. Again drawing on the early history of the Church, he looked to the period before Joseph Smith's death, when the Apostles were endowed with the keys of the Kingdom of God. In his theology, the kingdom is "God's political government on earth, having within its functions the protection of all people, whether members of the Church of Christ or not. This Kingdom, with Christ the King, is destined to subjugate all other kingdoms and rule the world."[28] Just as the Church is the "spiritual branch or propaganda division" of the priesthood, the kingdom is entrusted with "guarding and administering God's Holy ordinances necessary to the salvation and exaltation of man."[29] The kingdom is a force of protection and government, operated by the priesthood, in the lives of believers.

Musser and his coauthor J. Leslie Broadbent argued in *Priesthood Items* that the Kingdom of God exists on earth. Joseph Smith established the Council of Fifty as a legislative organization that sought to establish Smith's theodemocratic vision on earth and prepare for the Millennium. In a time of heightened persecution against the young Church, the council brought together "honest and honorable men, not members of the Church, but rightful citizens of the Kingdom, who, as it was their duty to do, championed the cause of the Church in the dark days of mob violence and drivings."[30] Among these men were the members of the Quorum of the Twelve Apostles, highlighting the sacred nature of the organization, despite its temporal mission. Under persecution and excommunication by President Grant, Musser applied the early history of the kingdom to his persecution, arguing that Grant and the institutional Church had no jurisdiction over his standing before God because they were merely the Church, not the priesthood or the Kingdom of God.[31]

Musser's vision for a twentieth-century Kingdom of God was never fully realized. With one exception, there is little evidence of a kingdom established by members of the priesthood council. In a 1952 diary entry, Joseph Lyman Jessop recorded the following:

> August G. M. Ostendorf was confirmed by R. C. Allred in about the following language: "Bro. (calling candidate by name), In the authority of the Holy Priesthood, we lay our hands upon your head and confirm you a member of the Church of Jesus Christ of Latter-day Saints and of the Kingdom of God.[32]

With no additional context, not much is known about this confirmation or the extent to which either Musser or Allred established a temporal organization other than the United Order. It became the case, however, that participation in the Kingdom of God was a prerequisite for attaining stewardships in the United Order. "Obviously only members of the Church in good standing (or, of course, of the Kingdom, which, in the broad sense, embraces the Church) are eligible for stewardships." The United Order was both part of the hierarchical structure of the priesthood and an access point for entry into the structure.[33]

Musser first wrote about the United Order as the economic law of heaven in 1938 and introduced the concept to polygamous Mormons as a vital part of the restored faith.[34] The early communitarian model was presented as contradictory to the Church's newly launched welfare program, which Musser argued bore "little or no resemblance to the order revealed from heaven."[35] In his overview of communitarian history, Musser took his readers back to February 1831 and the revelation that became canonized as Doctrine and Covenants 42: "And behold, thou wilt remember the poor and consecrate of thy properties for their support that which thou hast to impart unto them, with a covenant and a deed which cannot be broken."[36] In the revelation, God revealed several aspects of the heavenly economic system: the faithful should remember the poor, bishops should handle consecration, each member should receive a stewardship, the excess should be kept in the storehouse and distributed to the poor, and what is left over should be saved for purchasing land that would build the New Jerusalem.[37]

To bring the vision of a United Order to fruition, Musser outlined five key features that work together to create an equitable system for the Saints: consecration, stewardship, tithing from income, tithing from surplus, and sacrifice. Within this framework, Musser affirmed what many past leaders had previously argued, that tithing is a "lesser law" that prepares the individual and family for consecration. Musser argued that the Church's present system of tithing and building storehouses for the poor was not only inadequate but unjust and no better than the world's system of taxation that left the poor in a financially precarious state. As he explained,

> Standing alone tithing would be an unjust law. It would tend to make the poor poorer without humbling the rich. As practiced in the Church today, it cannot be other than discriminatory and unjust. It taxes the wage-earner who gets but $40, $50 or $60 per month, often not enough to furnish the bare necessities for his family, at the same rate as it taxes

the man whose earnings reach from $500 to $10,000 or more per month, and whose actual needs are far below such income. Generally speaking, men of large incomes have small families, while those of small incomes have the larger families. One receiving $1,000 per month can more easily live on the $900 remaining after the payment of the 10 per cent tithing, than can his neighbor whose salary is only $50 per month. The $5 he pays in tithing from his pittance may spell the difference between wearing shoes and going bare-foot; child labor or schooling; in fact, existence or starvation. Such a law, standing alone, works injustices. Indeed, under the strict rule of tithing, divested of the other features of the United Order, a rich man may be entirely relieved from paying tithing and yet be a member of the Church in good standing.[38]

To address the disparity that tithing perpetuates between the wealthy and the poor, Musser argued for surplus tithing. He explained, "The principle of tithing the tenth reaches all men blessed with earning power, making workers of them in the great gospel hive, while a portion of them may be so blessed as to be able to pay into the treasury of the Lord both a tenth and a surplus. From this view-point tithing the tenth as well as the surplus is seen to be a most wise provision."[39]

On its own, tithing perpetuates inequality and does not serve to benefit the whole. Only once all people renounce private interests and hold all things in common through full consecration can Mormons attain Zion and be counted as the "pure in heart."[40] Unlike the LDS Church's tithing system, Musser framed consecration as an alternative that begins with the understanding that everything belongs to God and that living communally is the best way to honor that reality:

Fundamentally the earth with all its contents belongs to God. It is His heritage. He organized it. This situation man agreed to in his pre-mortal existence. Such agreement was his passport into mortality. Jesus Christ inherits the earth through obedience to the laws of his Father—they are to become joint owners. Men may also become joint owners with them through obedience to their laws. Meantime, man is a lessee. He operates under sanction. His lands, herds, silver, gold, homes, children and wives—all he is possessed of, belong to God. Within the United Order system, a stewardship was awarded to a consecrator.[41]

Enoch, the Old Testament Patriarch who was assumed into Heaven after a righteous life and established a city that incorporated God's economic and political structure exemplified God's economic and political structure. In Musser's account of the United Order's history, it was Enoch's system that was replicated by leaders in the Church, with subsequent failures attributed to "human selfishness and a disinclination on the part of the Saints to grasp the full significance of the movement."[42] In short, the economic system is perfect, but the Latter-day Saints are not. Enoch's system was created by and for consecrated people. Through the system, participants were perfected to the point of translation, changed from a mortal to an immortal state without passing through death. The only problem was the human fallibility and stubbornness that failed to reach full consecration.

In Latter-day Saint economic theology, the United Order was necessary for Enoch to attain a perfected state. His example allowed others to participate in the same system as "an eternal law and qualifies for a celestial existence with the Gods."[43] The United Order was such a requirement that Musser went as far as to claim that "the Lord will starve the people into joining the United Order, which is the only economic law of heaven that will save His people."[44] Recalling one man's testimony about the United Order, he wrote,

> Bro. Owen stated it had been demonstrated to him he could not succeed temporally except thru the spirit of the United Order, and he was ready to turn in all he had, permitting the Priesthood to handle the same as they saw fit. He recognized those of the Great High Priests as being the mouthpiece of God on the earth. He classed the present world and the people as Telestial beings, catering to the physical desires. Those who were rising above this sphere were in the Terrestrial life, where intellectuality predominated, and were learning to eat to live, rather than live to eat. Having reached this point, some were reaching out for the celestial where all earthly ills and mistakes will be overcome.[45]

To have a testimony in Mormonism was to have a testimony in its economic order. It was part and parcel of a religious system where each component was inextricably linked. After a 1935 priesthood meeting that discussed the United Order at length, he summarized this reality: "Had pleasant time with family, and bore testimony that the next move is United Order. Order of Abraham cannot be fully lived without the order of Enoch; and that many of the brethren would be offended at the Priesthood and would be sorely tried over this matter."[46]

As in his perspective on polygamy, Musser centered his criticism of the Church as an institution that too quickly comported with the American economic system, abandoning a system given by God for the greater welfare of the Latter-day Saints:

> There is no logic whatever in a single Latter-day Saint being upon the "relief" roles in the present depression and yet while latest reports show the majority of the States improving in this respect Utah is gaining in its relief contributions. Were the Saints invited in a practical way to join a United Order move, such as the Church with its vast resources could inaugurate, they would do so readily and joyously. We could well afford to sell our hotels, and build less meeting houses, if necessary, to acquire funds, to place the people in business, on farms, etc. Such would eventually, besides supporting themselves, begin to return revenue back into the coffers of the Church. From an investment point of view alone, it would pay. The leaders must, if they would succeed, say less and do more.[47]

By advocating the government's economic system, the Church cast aside its history and the people who sought to protect the family structure inaugurated by Joseph Smith. In contrast, the polygamous Mormons advocated the truest method of livelihood, "We are advancing preparation for the setting of the house of God in order, by teaching the United Order, the Patriarchal Order and other principles of the Gospel, and washing away the 'refuge of lies' behind which the brethren have been hiding for some years."[48]

In the same way that Mormon cosmology reimagined sacrifice as the avenue for heavenly blessings, the choice to live United Order and faithfully accept its responsibilities "leads to an inheritance in eternity."[49] To choose the contrary was an impossibility:

> This system of stewardship is the natural, God-inspired order of financial, economic, and industrial life, and until we set up this order we shall experience NOTHING but trouble, war, revolution, mobocracy, financial ruin, poverty and general depression; the present debacle will continue and grow worse until leaders see the light and step out of the beaten paths of error and resolve to save the people by the one and only effective means. So natural, so nearly perfect, so sure, and so saving is this system of stewardship that God himself and His Son Jesus saw fit to reveal it and set it up among men for their temporal salvation. How and why shall we question it in the face of these facts? It must and will come. How long shall we stand in its way? HOW IT WOULD LIFT AND

EXALT US FROM THE PITS WE HAVE DIGGED FOR OURSELVES IN OUR
FINANCIAL BABYLON.[50]

In the minds of the faithful Mormons who sought to establish and live
the United Order, the institutional Church that renounced polygamy also
renounced the only economic system supported by God. They not only
sought to appease the world in their kinship networks but also in the realm
of their livelihoods. To be thoroughly American was to be middle-class
and participate in the economy. The choice to abstain from this marker of
American life was to retain the mark of difference that became synonymous
with the Mormons who settled on the Arizona Strip.

In 1935, as the polygamous Mormons finalized their plans to establish
the United Order, Musser wrote the following of the preparations made for
the community that became known as Short Creek, the settlement on the
border between Utah and Arizona that became synonymous with polygamy
throughout the twentieth century:

> On 11th, spent day at home of Bro. Owens in Union Dist. 40 acres which
> he asks the privilege of putting in a cooperative movement looking
> toward the establishment of the United Order. He wants no guarantees
> or promises, but recognizing the Priesthood as he does, is prepared to
> give over everything to them. Presidents Barlow, Kelsch and myself went
> over the farm carefully. Following are condensed facts:
>
> 40 acres—30 irrigable. 30 shares water, market value $70. each.
> Reservoir sight [sic], easily adapted for 10
>
> Present crop:
> Two A. contract peas
> Abt. one acre garden peas for drying
> 1/2 acre contract beans
> Some old fruit trees and abt. 125 new trees, cherries, apples, peaches,
> pears, apricots—65 cherry trees. Raspberry bushes and strawberries and
> some plums. Has alfalfa and corn planted.
> Splendid place for grape. Some vines yielding.
> Brick house, 7 rooms and bath. Cistern with running water, electricity.
>
> Indebtedness:
> $2,600, at 6% being paid $13, per month (which is amount only of inter-
> est) Payments doubled beginning July 1, 1936. Just planted 2,000 tomato
> plants with help of Priesthood and brethren.[51]

The Priesthood Council selected Ianthus W. Barlow, Joseph Lyman Jessop, and Carl E. Jentzsch as the men set apart to establish the settlement and prepare the land for the United Order. Musser records that these men were "instructed to proceed to Short Creek, accept the leadership of Bro. Price W. Johnson, and not to drive a nail or saw a board, or engage in any occupation except under the influence of the Spirit of the Lord. Not to have their minds on money, but upon the glory of God."[52]

Of Barlow, Jessop, and Jentzsch's calling, Musser explained, "The brethren felt splendid and covenanted to carry out instructions. The Spirit tells me that this move is the beginning of the re-establishing of the United Order, and that though it has a very small beginning, it will grow to fill the whole earth."[53] Musser hoped that the Short Creek community would become a beacon of hope for both disenfranchised Mormons and people who remained in a state of financial difficulty in the Church. While the land selected for the operation was practical, spiritual meaning was imbued into the soil. Already in 1933, Lorin C. Woolley spoke of the Arizona Strip as divinely chosen: "The section near Lee's Ferry in Arizona is the hub of this intermountain country between Yucatan City and Canada. It was set apart under the direction of Brigham Young by John W. Woolley for the gathering of the Saints. It is a choice land."[54] Adding to the mythology of the land, Woolley declared, "In the Lee's Ferry section of Arizona, is the principle [sic] place where Jesus met the Nephite people after his resurrection."[55] For all these reasons, Short Creek was the obvious place to gather the faithful.

Musser's own experience in Short Creek was short-lived. While he established much of the historical and theological support for the community, he remained in northern Utah and handed the daily management of the community to John Y. Barlow. Under Barlow, the priesthood held power to include or exclude members as they saw fit, ultimately leading to tension in the community and consolidation of both spiritual and temporal power around the head of the priesthood. This model of priesthood was solidified under the leadership of Barlow's successor, LeRoy S. Johnson, and later, Rulon T. Jeffs. During Johnson's and Jeffs's tenures, the tension between the polygamous community and the outside world only grew, resulting in an infamous raid on the community in 1953 that increased retrenchment and isolation.

Musser's dream of an idyllic United Order, away from the watchful eye of the LDS Church and the state, ended with a controversial transfer of asserts. The United Effort Plan no longer exists in our day as a religious organization but was reorganized into a trust in 2006 by the Third Judicial District Court of Salt Lake County, Utah. The state reorganization took hold of all public streets, parks, schools, church meetinghouses, and cemeteries. The trust provides housing without discrimination based on religion, something counter to the theological foundations of the community. For the faithful who remain in Short Creek, refusing to comply with the demands of the new state-led trust, Musser's goal of a stable livelihood under the jurisdiction of divine law remains a distant hope.

Bibliographic Essay

From 1933 to the time he died in 1954, Joseph W. Musser devoted his time to writing and promoting Mormon history and doctrine. His pamphlets and periodicals laid the foundation for Mormon fundamentalism, a diverse group who believed they were the most authentic expression of the nineteenth-century faith. Toward the end of his life, he reflected on the designation *fundamentalist*, proclaiming, "We are called 'Fundamentalists' and are proud of the designation, signifying as it does, that we are clinging to the original Gospel as established by the Lord through His Prophet, Joseph Smith."[1] Even today, his writings continue to be among fundamentalism's most influential theological and apologetic works. Many current expressions of the Mormon fundamentalist movement, such as the Apostolic United Brethren, the Righteous Branch of the Church of Jesus Christ of Latter-day Saints, and the Church of the Firstborn, among others, trace their lineage to Musser's leadership and doctrinal development. Even among groups that do not hold a direct lineage to Musser's priesthood ordinations, his life is remembered for its devotion to the fundamentals of the gospel. I am hopeful that this overview of Musser's written work demonstrates the importance of his intellectual contribution to the development of a Mormonism not bound to the institutional Church and offers readers a starting point for further research.

Musser's diaries are housed in the Church History Library of the Church of Jesus Christ of Latter-day Saints, and much of his correspondence remains in private collections. Because of restricted access, they are not available to the public. Readers interested in Musser's life can, however, find a starting point in his published sermons and autobiography. One of the most significant sites for those interested in Musser's published work and other important writings that contributed to the fundamentalist movement is the wealth of primary resources at https://mormonpolygamydocuments. org, compiled by Brian Hales and Don Bradley. Hales and Bradley worked tirelessly to make the primary documents of the faith accessible to the public. The collection includes pamphlets, journals, and a complete collection of *Truth* magazine. Original versions of Musser's pamphlets remain in circulation and spread internationally in reprinted formats.

Periodicals

The Mormon fundamentalist movement began as an unorganized group of excommunicated, institutionally disciplined, and disillusioned Mormons who no longer recognized their Church. In the early years of the faith's development, ideas circulated in the homes of members who organized Sunday school and sacrament meetings to replicate their lost religious experiences. As interest grew, evangelizing the movement's message became increasingly crucial to its members, for the sake of both the gospel and their personal vindication. *Truth* was Musser's response to the growing needs of the community. In August 1933, Musser conceived the idea for the magazine in the hope that he "may get affairs in shape to begin publishing the truth."[2] With no employment, Musser devoted the next several years to ministry and preparing a series of pamphlets. In April 1935, the dream of a monthly periodical came to fruition, "TRUTH: Decided, with approval of my brethren, to begin the publication of a monthly magazine to be designated, Truth. This venture has been a dream for a long time, and I feel I am being lead [sic] properly in entertaining the desire and determination to begin this publication. It will be for the sole purpose of building up the kingdom of God."[3]

From 1935 to 1956, the twenty-one volumes of *Truth* magazine circulated to provide general audiences with a history of the fundamentalist movement and its doctrines. Many of Musser's most widely circulated pamphlets originated as editorials in *Truth*. "I have spent the year, championing the rights of the Priesthood, as against the arbitrary (as I see it actions and rule of the Church[)]. The TRUTH magazine has been the medium I have used. My brethren of the Priesthood Council have stood by me. If I have missed the mark, it has been innocent and entirely unintentional," he wrote in reflecting on his apologetic work in the ministry.[4] The publication covered topics that set the movement apart from the LDS Church, such as the continuation of polygamy, a distinct priesthood lineage, the Adam-God Doctrine, and the Law of Consecration. Musser served as editor, compiling quotes and sermons from LDS leaders that supported the movement's theological claims. The magazine included a monthly editorial by Musser that highlighted current events and exhorted the faithful. Never one to lose his focus on the institution and its perceived foibles, *Truth* always included biannual commentaries on the LDS Church's semiannual conference. During his prison sentence, Musser gave the editorial rights to his son, Guy Musser. After his father's release from prison, Guy refused to return the editorial position to his father. The tension in their relationship never resolved, and Musser began *Star of Truth* as a continuation of his work, a publication that ran under Musser's leadership for four issues. After his death, Guy Musser claimed editorial ownership of *Star of Truth*, which ran for forty issues after the initial four published by Musser.

Musser, Joseph W. *Truth*, vols. 1–21 (Salt Lake City: Truth Publishing, 1935–56).
———. *Star of Truth*, vols. 1–4 (Salt Lake City: Truth Publishing, 1953–56).

Pamphlets

Musser witnessed one of the most significant changes in the history of the LDS Church, the transition to a strictly monogamous faith and participation in the broader American religious landscape. Amid these changes, he witnessed families struggling to find their place within the institution that once promoted and solemnized their plural families. For this reason, Musser's first pamphlet was *The New and Everlasting Covenant of Marriage*, an overview of the Mormon marriage system and its continual importance to the Saints.[5] Truth Publishing Company initially released a hundred copies under the title Musser received through prayer. His largely apologetic pamphlets focused on presenting a continuity of faith and an unbroken chain of authority. Therefore, most of his time was spent compiling quotes from past Church leaders and offering brief commentaries to support his position.

While a majority of the pamphlets focused on the differentiation between the priesthood and the Church in an attempt to support continuing the practice of plural marriage, he also offered insight into the nature of God, consecration, and the end times. The pamphlets sought to make sense of a changing religious institution that no longer valued the sacrifices of those who continued the more challenging parts of the faith. At the same time, they justified Musser's position outside the Church and expressed his deeply held doctrinal convictions. For all his struggles, a lack of faith in the Mormon Restoration was never among them. Each pamphlet highlighted the ambiguous relationship with Mormonism that many experienced after their excommunication and offered consolation to the families who followed his counsel.

Musser, Joseph W. *Celestial or Plural Marriage: A Digest of the Mormon Marriage System as Established by God through the Prophet Joseph Smith* (Salt Lake City: Truth Publishing, 1944).
———. *The Coming Crisis* (Salt Lake City: Truth Publishing, 1943).
———. *The Economic Order of Heaven* (Salt Lake City: Truth Publishing, 1948).
———. *Four Hidden Revelations* (Salt Lake City: Truth Publishing, 1948).
———. *The Law of Plural Marriage* (Salt Lake City: Truth Publishing, 1948).
———. *Michael, Our Father and Our God* (Salt Lake City: Truth Publishing, 1938).
———. *The New and Everlasting Covenant of Marriage* (Salt Lake City: Truth Publishing, 1933).
———. *A Priesthood Issue* (Salt Lake City: Truth Publishing, 1948).
———. *Priesthood Items* (Salt Lake City: Truth Publishing, 1934).
———. *Supplement to the New and Everlasting Covenant of Marriage* (Salt Lake City: Truth Company, 1934).

Personal Writings

Musser is best known through his daily diary entries and letters between leaders of the LDS Church and the Mormon fundamentalist movement. Through these documents, readers are afforded a glimpse into the lived experience of polygamy's end. The First and Second Manifestos did not create a clear demarcation of the time before and after polygamy. Nowhere is this more evident than in the lives of the men and women who continued the practice of plural marriage after the institutional end to the practice. The personal diaries and correspondence of the men and women who continued plural marriage after the manifestos demonstrate how Musser's life, and the lives of his followers, became foils by which the LDS Church understood its new place as a fully American religion. In addition to his personal records, Musser wrote an autobiography in which he reflected on his life and his relationship with the Church. The autobiography, written late in life, offers a more skeptical and harsher retrospect than his daily diaries portray. The tension between the institution and the disaffected Mormons shows clearly in Musser's reflections.

Lorin C. Woolley, the man who ordained Musser as a High Priest Apostle after his excommunication from the LDS Church, did not keep a diary or any written records. The early intellectual tradition of the movement remains through the pen of Musser, however, who kept a detailed record of Woolley's sermons and priesthood meetings. More than intellectual history, his record offers insight into the mind of an early believer in the fundamentalist movement. Woolley's sermons were a way to make sense of personal and professional difficulties. For Musser, they were a source of hope for those among Mormonism's most disaffected.

Briney, Drew, ed. *Joseph W. Musser's Book of Remembrances* (n.p.: Hindsight, 2010).

Musser, Joseph W. *Autobiography and Journals of Saint Joseph White Musser (1929–1949): A Brief Sketch of the Life, Labors and Faith of Saint Joseph White Musser* (n.p.: n.d.)

———. *Book of Remembrances* (1939). Unpublished ms., transcribed and edited by Bryan Buchanan. Photocopy in author's possession.

———. *Woolley School of the Prophets Meeting Minutes (1934–1941)*. Unpublished ms., transcribed and edited by Bryan Buchanan. Photocopies in author's possession.

Taylor, Nathan, and Bonnie Taylor, eds. *The Sermons of Joseph W. Musser, 1940–1945*. 2 vols., 2nd ed. Edited by Nathan and Bonnie Taylor (n.p.: Messenger Publications, 2004–8).

Notes

Chapter One. Saint Joseph White Musser

1. The form of Musser's name alternates between Joseph White Musser and Saint Joseph White Musser throughout his life. While not listed on his birth or death certificate, "Saint" is listed as an alternate name on the Church History Biographical Database, https://history.churchofjesuschrist.org/chd/individual /saint-joseph-white-musser-1872. "Saint" is a commonly used name for the late leader of the fundamentalist movement, but it always is considered more than a mere honorific. In a comment made during the 2022 annual meeting of the Mormon History Association, David G. Watson, the president of the priesthood of the Apostolic United Brethren, noted that "Saint" was the name used during Musser's christening, https://mormonhistoryassociation .org/landscape-art-religion-mha-2022/5k-approaches-to-mormon-thought-a -roundtable-discussion/.

2. "Patriarchal Blessing of St. Joseph White Musser, July 17, 1902," photocopy in author's possession.

3. Susan Friend Harding, *The Book of Jerry Falwell: Fundamentalist Language and Politics* (Princeton, NJ: Princeton University Press, 2001); Seth Dowland, *Family Values and the Rise of the Christian Right* (Philadelphia: University of Pennsylvania Press, 2015); J. Michael Utzinger, *Yet Saints Their Watch Are Keeping: Fundamentalist, Modernists, and the Development of Evangelical Ecclesiology, 1887–1937* (Macon, GA: Mercer University Press, 2006); Joel Carpenter, *Revive Us Again: The Reawakening of American Fundamentalism* (New York: Oxford University Press, 1999).

4. John Lardas Modern, *Secularism in Antebellum America* (Chicago: University of Chicago Press), 74.

5. Audio of these comments is available through the Mormon History 2022 Annual Meeting during the "Approaches to Mormon Thought: A Round-

table Discussion" panel, https://mormonhistoryassociation.org/landscape
-art-religion-mha-2022/5k-approaches-to-mormon-thought-a-roundtable
-discussion/.

6. Joseph White Musser, *Autobiography and Journals of Saint Joseph White Musser (1929–1949): A Brief Sketch of the Life, Labors and Faith of Saint Joseph White Musser,* n.p. n.d., 8. Photocopy in author's possession.

7. Musser, *Autobiography,* 4.

8. "Official Declaration 1," October 6, 1890, https://www.churchofjesuschrist.org/study/scriptures/dc-testament/od/1?lang=eng.

9. Joseph W. Musser, Journal, November 7, 1895, Journals, 1895–1911, MS1862, Church History Library. See also Patrick Mason, *The Mormon Menace: Violence and Anti-Mormonism in the Postbellum South* (Oxford: Oxford University Press, 2011).

10. Musser, Journal, January 10, 1987.

11. Musser, Journal, January 30, 1897.

12. Musser, Journal, November 30, 1899.

13. Musser, Journal, November 30, 1899.

14. Musser, *Autobiography,* 9.

15. Musser, *Autobiography,* 9.

16. William B. Smart, *Mormonism's Last Colonizer: The Life and Times of William H. Smart* (Logan: Utah State University Press, 2008), 113.

17. Musser, Journal, May 30, 1901.

18. Musser, Journal, November 17, 1901

19. Through this calling, Musser became reacquainted with Louis A. Kelsch, the former president of the Northern States mission, whom Musser met while serving in the Southern States mission. Kelsch and Musser eventually served a prison sentence together after the 1944 raid on the polygamists in southern Utah. Today, Kelsch is best known as the father of the independent Mormon fundamentalist movement.

20. Musser, *Autobiography,* 8.

21. For more on postmanifesto polygamy, see D. Michael Quinn, "LDS Church Authority and New Plural Marriages, 1890–1904," *Dialogue* 18, no. 1 (Spring 1985): 9–105, Brian Hales, *Modern Polygamy and Mormon Fundamentalism: The Generations after the Manifesto* (Salt Lake City: Greg Kofford, 2006), and Craig L. Foster and Marianne T. Watson, *American Polygamy: A History of Fundamentalist Mormon* Faith (Charleston, SC: History Press, 2019), 85.

22. Musser, Journal, October 16, 1902.

23. Musser, Journal, May 26, 1902.

24. Musser, Journal, November 1, 1901.

25. "Letter to Joseph White Musser from Reed Smoot, March 2, 1908." Photocopy in author's possession.

26. "1904 Statement by Joseph F. Smith" (April 1904), https://www. churchofjesuschrist.org/topics/plural-marriage-and-families-in-early-utah/ joseph-f-smith-statement?lang=eng.

27. Musser, Journal, April 6, 1904.

28. Musser, Journal, April 10, 1904.

29. "Judson Tolman Sealing Record Signed by Judson Tolman on February 7, 1912." Photocopy in author's possession.

30. Tolman's personal sealings included Sarah Holbrook (1846), Mary Reeves (1852), Sophia Merrell (1856), Zibiah Stoker (1869), Eleanor Odd (1906), and Marie Forsman (1906).

31. Doctrine and Covenants 124:93.

32. Heber J. Grant, *Conference Report*, April 1921, 220; James R. Clark, ed., *Messages of the First Presidency* (Salt Lake City: Bookcraft, 1965–71), 5: 196.

33. Musser, *Autobiography*, 10.

34. "Was the Manifesto a Revelation?," *Truth* 1, no. 7 (December 1935): 82.

35. Musser, Journal, July 22, 1909.

36. Musser, Journal, July 22, 1909.

37. Kathleen Flake, *The Politics of American Religious Identity: The Seating of Senator Reed Smoot, Mormon Apostle* (Chapel Hill: University of North Carolina Press, 2004), 56—81.

38. Musser, Journal, July 22, 1909.

39. Musser, Journal, July 22, 1909. Both men were eventually excommunicated in 1911.

40. Musser, Journal, July 22, 1909.

41. Smart first approached Musser to practice consecration in 1902. On September 16 of that year, Musser documented with the note "In evening, Met Prest. Smart, who came up from Salt Lake. We had a long talk of our personal affair. He invited me to join him in attempting to live the 'United Order,' which invitation I gratefully accepted. The details of our plan will be worked out later" (Musser, Journal, September 16, 1902). The following day, the men and their families met to discuss the details of a "community of interests." "He spoke at length about the possibilities in the Patriarchal form of Marriage, going from that to the principle of the 'United' Order. His desire for years had been to live this grand principle, that he might receive experience + development + be in a position to serve the Lord with more purpose. He expressed a willingness to turn his property in to a common fund, which should receive the efforts of those belonging to the order. An expression was taken, + those present agreed to enter into such an understanding that the principle involves. The question of establishing an educational home at Provo + concentrating our efforts at economy + family union along lines which we have individually talked over was discussed. It was unanimously agreed to leave this matter to the judgment

+ good wisdom of the husbands involved + to follow their direction as they shall feel impressed of the Lord" (Musser, Journal, September 17, 1902).

42. Musser, Journal, July 22, 1909.

43. Musser, Journal, July 22, 1909.

44. Musser, Journal, July 22, 1909.

45. Family stories attest that Musser recorded some journal-like notes during the interim period.

46. Musser, *Autobiography*, 10. While "the Apostle" has been associated with Brigham Young Jr., that is an impossibility because Young died in 1903. Musser does not name the Apostle in his writings.

47. Musser, *Autobiography*, 10

48. Musser, Journal, February 23, 1921.

49. Musser, Journal, March 12, 1921.

50. Musser, Journal, March 12, 1921.

51. Musser, Journal, March 23, 1921.

52. Musser, Journal, March 23, 1921.

53. Marianne T. Watson, "Short Creek: 'A Refuge for the Saints,'" *Dialogue* 36, no. 1 (Spring 2003): 75.

54. Flake, *Politics of American Religious Identity*.

55. Musser, Journal, July 25, 1921.

56. Musser, Journal, May 17, 1921.

57. Musser, Journal, May 26, 1921.

58. Musser, Journal, May 26, 1921.

59. Merrill Singer, "Nathaniel Baldwin, Utah Inventor and Patron of the Fundamentalist Movement" *Utah Historical Quarterly* 47, no. 1 (November 1979): 42–53. In 1922, Baldwin proclaimed himself the "One Mighty and Strong" (alluding to D&C 85), a term used within the Mormon fundamentalist movement to denote authority to lead the movement.

60. Nathaniel Baldwin, Journal, August 28, 1921, in Nathaniel Baldwin Journals, June 1921–December 1922, MS 12783, LDS Church History Library.

61. *Woolley School of the Prophets Meeting Minutes*, transcribed and edited by Bryan Buchanan, 1. Photocopies in author's possession.

62. *Woolley School of the Prophets Meeting Minutes*, 4.

63. Lorin C. Woolley, "Statement of Facts," 1912. Photocopy in author's possession. During the postmanifesto period, "the underground" became a metaphor for efforts to evade federal officials.

64. Woolley, "Statement of Facts." Later accounts of the 1886 Revelation include Jesus Christ at the visitation alongside Joseph Smith.

65. Woolley, "Statement of Facts."

66. Musser, Journal, March 12, 1922.

67. Musser, Journal, March 12, 1922.

68. Musser, Journal, March 12, 1922.

69. Musser, Journal, March 12, 1922.

70. Baldwin, Journal, April 9, 1922. Baldwin recorded that fifty people were in attendance at the meeting.

71. Baldwin, Journal, April 9, 1922.

72. Baldwin, Journal, April 9, 1922.

73. Baldwin, Journal, April 9, 1922.

74. Baldwin, Journal, April 9, 1922.

75. Baldwin, Journal, April 9, 1922. There is no evidence that Lorin C. Woolley helped write the Woodruff Manifesto.

76. Alluding to Moses 7:18.

77. Musser, Journal, March 15, 1922.

78. Musser, Journal, March 16, 1921.

79. Musser, Journal, March 8, 1922.

80. Musser, Journal, August 27, 1922.

81. Musser, Journal, September 1, 1922.

82. Musser, Journal, September 1, 1922. Again, Musser cast blame on those who "deluded" Mary and convinced her of the fault in plural marriage.

83. Musser, Journal, September 1, 1922. At the same time, Musser was increasingly estranged from his son, Neil, who left the LDS Church for the Methodist Episcopal Church as an adult (Musser, Journal, March 21, 1922).

84. Musser, *Autobiography*, 19.

85. In Latter-day Saint theology, the "One Mighty and Strong" is a title associated with Doctrine and Covenants 85 to describe a figure prophesied to return at the end of time to "set in order the house of God" (D&C 85:7). See also Brian C. Hales, "John T. Clark: The 'One Mighty and Strong,'" *Dialogue* 39, no. 3 (Fall 2006): 46–63. Musser first heard Clark's claim as the One Mighty and Strong through a mutual friend in July 1931.

86. Hales, "John T. Clark," 47.

87. Hales, "John T. Clark," 50.

88. Musser, Journal, June 14, 1922.

89. Musser, Journal, June 14, 1922.

90. In a journal entry, Musser clarified the view that an Apostle is an individual who has witnessed the resurrected Jesus Christ, while a Seventy is one who offers a witness on behalf of the resurrected Jesus Christ, without a direct visitation (Musser, Journal, April 9, 1922). After the 1886 meeting, many of the men involved in the telling of the history claimed a direct witness and special authority from that interaction.

91. Musser, Journal, May 14, 1929.

92. Musser, *Autobiography*, 11.

93. Musser, Journal, March 8, 1933.

94. Musser, Journal, November 30, 1930.

95. Musser, Journal, April 4, 1931.

96. Musser, Journal, April 4, 1931.

97. Musser, Journal, April 4, 1931.

98. Musser, Journal, April 20, 1931.

99. Musser, Journal, April 20, 1931.

100. Amos Kmetzsch Musser, "Biography of Lucile Ottilie Kmetzsch," in Gertrude M. Richards collection, 1861–1984, MS 12733, LDS Church History Library.

101. Musser, "Lucy Ottilie Kmetzsch Musser," 4.

102. Musser, Journal, October 22, 1934.

103. Musser, Journal, October 22, 1934.

104. Brian Hales, "'I Have Been Fanatically Religious': Joseph White Musser, Father of the Fundamentalist Movement," presented at the May 1993 Mormon History Association meeting in St. George, Utah.

105. Musser, Journal, September 30, 1930.

106. *Woolley School of the Prophets Meeting Minutes*, 60.

107. Musser, Journal, September 10, 1933.

108. Musser, Journal, July 26, 1934. Myrtle's sisters were also involved in the fundamentalist movement. Her sister, Mary Viola Anderson, married within the movement and gave birth to Lynn Thompson, the late leader of the Apostolic United Brethren.

109. Anne Wilde uses the term in her interview with Rick Bennett on *Gospel Tangents* (Rick C. Bennet, host, "Third Manifesto Causes Schism: Apostolic United Brethren," *Gospel Tangents* [podcast], October 31, 2017, https://gospeltangents.com/2017/10/31/third-manifesto-causes-schism-apostolic-united-brethren/).

110. "Official Statement on Plural Marriage, June 17, 1933," in *Messages of the First Presidency*, vol. 5, comp. James R. Clark (Salt Lake City: Bookcraft, 1971), 315.

111. "Official Statement on Plural Marriage," 315.

112. "Official Statement on Plural Marriage," 315.

113. "Official Statement on Plural Marriage," 316.

114. Musser, Journal, July 1, 1933.

115. Musser, Journal, July 1, 1933.

116. Musser, Journal, August 8, 1933.

117. Musser, Journal, August 8, 1933.

118. "Announcement," *Truth* 1, no. 1 (June 1, 1935): 1.

119. Musser, Journal, September 27, 1933.

120. Musser, Journal, September 11, 1933.

121. Musser, Journal, April 29, 1941.

122. Musser, Journal, March 12, 1934.

123. Musser, Journal, July 19, 1937.

124. Musser, Journal, September 19, 1934.

125. Musser, Journal, September 19, 1934.

126. Watson, "Short Creek," 86.

127. Watson, "Short Creek," 79.

128. "The Short Creek Embroglio," *Truth* 1, no. 5 (October 1, 1935): 51.

129. "The Short Creek Embroglio," *Truth* 1, no. 5 (October 1, 1935): 51.

130. "Letter to Joseph White Musser from Heber J. Grant," November 27, 1928. Photocopy in author's possession.

131. "Youth's Solemn Protest," *Truth* 1, no. 9 (February 1, 1936): 121.

132. Musser, Journal, November 8, 1936. One-man rule ultimately became a defining feature of the Short Creek community, later organized as the Fundamentalist Church of Jesus Christ of Latter Day Saints under LeRoy S. Johnson. The autocracy led to schism within the community, resulting in the formation of Centennial Park under Alma Timpson and Marion Hammon.

133. Musser, Journal, November 8, 1936.

134. Musser, Journal, November 13, 1936.

135. Musser, Journal, November 22, 1938.

136. Musser, *Autobiography*, 16.

137. Byron Harvey Allred, *A Leaf in Review: Of the Words and Arts of God and Men Relative to the Fullness of the Gospel* (Caldwell, ID: Caxton, 1933).

138. Elisa Eastwood Pudillo, *The Spiritual Evolution of Margarito Bautisa: Mexican Mormon Evangelizer, Polygamist, Dissident, and Utopian Founder, 1878–1961* (New York: Oxford University Press, 2020).

139. Melba F. Allred, "Sunday Evening, May 15, 1966, Items concerning Priesthood," in *Gems*, comp. Gilbert A. Fulton Jr (Salt Lake City: Gems, 1967), 33.

140. M. Allred, "Sunday Evening, May 15, 1966, Items concerning Priesthood," 33.

141. M. Allred, "Sunday Evening, May 15, 1966, Items concerning Priesthood," 33.

142. M. Allred, "Sunday Evening, May 15, 1966, Items concerning Priesthood," 34.

143. M. Allred, "Sunday Evening, May 15, 1966, Items concerning Priesthood," 34.

144. Melba F. Allred, Journal, October 29, 1950, Samuel W. Taylor collection, MS 10568, LDS Church History Library, 118.

145. M. Allred, "Sunday Evening, May 15, 1966, Items concerning Priesthood," 35.

146. M. Allred, "Sunday Evening, May 15, 1966, Items concerning Priesthood," 35.

147. M. Allred, "Sunday Evening, May 15, 1966, Items concerning Priesthood," 41.

148. "Saint Joseph White Musser, In Memoriam," *Truth* 20, no. 1 (June 1954): 1–48.

149. "Saint Joseph White Musser, In Memoriam," *Truth* 20, no. 1 (June 1954): 35.

150. "Saint Joseph White Musser, In Memoriam," *Truth* 20, no. 1 (June 1954): 34.

151. "Saint Joseph White Musser, In Memoriam," *Truth* 20, no. 1 (June 1954): 34–36.

152. Musser, Journal, July 28, 1940.

Chapter Two. The Order Pertaining to the Ancient of Days

1. David John Buerger, "'The Fulness of the Priesthood': The Second Anointing in Latter-day Saint Theology and Practice," *Dialogue* 16, no. 1 (1983): 10–44.

2. *A Priesthood Issue* (Salt Lake City: Truth Publishing, 1948), 1.

3. Joseph W. Musser, "Sermon, April 6, 1941," in *The Sermons of Joseph W. Musser, 1940–1945, Vols 1 and 2*, 2nd ed., edited by Nathan and Bonnie Taylor (n.p.: Messenger Publications, 2004–8), 46.

4. "Comments on the Mormon Marriage System," *Truth* 3, no. 1 (June 1, 1937): 25.

5. Brigham Young, *Journal of Discourses*, April 9, 1852, 26 vols. (London: LDS Booksellers, 1846–86), 1: 46.

6. Joseph W. Musser, *Michael, Our Father and Our God: The Mormon Conception of Deity as Taught by Joseph Smith, Brigham Young, John Taylor and Their Associates in the Priesthood*, 4th ed. (Salt Lake City: Truth Publishing, 1963), 100.

7. Musser, *Michael, Our Father and Our God*, 109.

8. Musser, *Michael, Our Father and Our God*, 75.

9. Musser, *Michael, Our Father and Our God*, 85.

10. Musser, *Michael, Our Father and Our God*, 43–45.

11. Musser, *Michael, Our Father and Our God*, 4.

12. "Joseph Smith, "The Witness and Testator," *Truth* 3, no. 7 (December 1937): 106.

13. *A Compendium of the Doctrines of the Gospel second edition*, compiled by Franklin D. Richard and Elder James A. Little (Salt Lake City: Deseret News, 1884), 1108.

14. "Joseph Smith, "The Witness and Testator," *Truth* 3, no. 7 (December 1937): 112.

15. Musser, "Sermon, March 28, 1943," in *Sermons*, 157.

16. "The Priesthood's Supremacy," *Truth* 2, no. 2 (July 1, 1936): 22.

17. James E. Talmage, *The Great Apostasy: Considered in the Light of Scriptural and Secular History* (Portland, OR: Northwestern States Mission, Church of Jesus Christ of Latter-Day Saints, 1909), i.

18. Talmage, *The Great Apostasy*, i.

19. Talmage, *The Great Apostasy*, i.

20. Musser, *Priesthood Issue*, 5.

21. "Does the Church Control the Priesthood?," *Truth* 4, no. 6 (November 1938): 112.

22. Musser, *Priesthood Issue*, 6.

23. Musser, *Priesthood Issue*, 6.

24. Musser, *Priesthood Issue*, 6.

25. Musser, *Priesthood Issue*, 6.

26. Brigham Young, May 7, 1861, *Journal of Discourses*, 9: 87.

27. Joseph Fielding Smith, *Doctrines of Salvation* (Salt Lake City: Bookcraft, 1954), 3: 154.

28. "I have not revoked the law nor will I for it is everlasting and those who will enter into my glory must obey the conditions thereof, even so, Amen." For a copy of the revelation, see Joseph W. Musser and J. Leslie Broadbent, *Supplement to the New and Everlasting Covenant of Marriage* (Salt Lake City: Truth Publishing, n.d.), 62–63.

29. Musser and Broadbent, *Supplement to the New and Everlasting Covenant*, 62–63.

30. After the end of the priesthood ban in 1978, some fundamentalists argued that the LDS Church lost all authority and a new Restoration was necessary. The True and Living Church of Jesus Christ of Saints of the Last Days in Manti, Utah, led by James D. Harmston, became emblematic of that position in the 1990s.

31. A. Nathan Boss, *The Sanhedrin* (n.p.: 1998). Photocopy in author's possession.

32. Historically, this day marks the first endowment ceremony in Nauvoo. Some scholars note that these men also signify the number of men needed for a quorum in Royal Arch Masonry. See, for example, Cheryl L. Bruno, Joe Steve Swick III, and Nicholas S. Literski, *Method Infinite: Freemasonry and the Mormon Restoration* (Salt Lake City: Greg Kofford, 2022), 332.

33. "History, 1838–1856," volume C-1 (2 November 1838–31 July 1842), p. 1328, Joseph Smith Papers, https://www.josephsmithpapers.org/paper-summary /history-1838-1856-volume-c-1-2-november-1838-31-july-1842/1/.

34. Entry of May 4, 1842, "History, 1838–1856."

35. Orson Pratt, September 7, 1879, *Journal of Discourses* (London: LDS Booksellers, 1854–86), 21: 133.

36. Musser, Journal, April 7, 1903.

37. John A. Widtsoe, "Evidences and Reconciliations," *Improvement Era* 43, no. 1 (February 1940): 97.

38. "Conference Reflections," *Truth* 5, no. 10 (March 1940): 284.

39. Buerger, "Fulness of the Priesthood," 40.

40. Buerger, "Fulness of the Priesthood," 40.

41. In *Michael, Our Father and Our God*, Musser argued that the Adam-God doctrine was not revealed to the entire Church but was a doctrine of priesthood. Similarly, polygamy was not meant for the entire Church but was a practice for the priesthood.

42. "Conference Notes," *Truth* 3, no. 1 (December 1937): 69.

43. "Is World Popularity Desirable? Conference Notes," *Truth* 2, no. 16 (November 1, 1936): 87.

44. "Was the Manifesto a Revelation?," *Truth* 1, no. 7 (December 1935): 82.

45. "Letter to the Presidency and High Council of Hyrum Stake of Zion," *Truth* 1, no. 10 (March 1, 1936): 129.

46. "Was the Manifesto a Revelation?," 82.

47. "Was the Manifesto a Revelation?," 82.

48. "Anniversary Number," *Truth* 3, no. 1 (December 1937): 8.

49. "Was the Manifesto a Revelation?," 82.

50. "Priesthood's Supremacy," *Truth* 2, no. 2 (July 1936): 25.

51. Musser, Journal, March 16, 1934.

52. Brian Hales, *Modern Polygamy and Mormon Fundamentalism: The Generations after the Manifesto* (Salt Lake City: Greg Kofford, 2006), 41.

53. Hales, *Modern Polygamy and Mormon Fundamentalism*, 41.

54. Hales, *Modern Polygamy and Mormon Fundamentalism*, 153. Hales cites Doctrine and Covenants 42:11 as the scriptural validation for ordinations outside the Church.

55. Jonathan Stapley, *The Power of Godliness: Mormon Liturgy and Cosmology* (New York: Oxford University Press, 2018), 15.

56. Jill Mulvay Derr and C. Brooklyn Derr, "'Outside the Mormon Hierarchy': Alternative Aspects of Institutional Power," *Dialogue* 15, no. 1 (Winter 1982): 23. See also Thomas Alexander, *Mormonism in Transition: A History of the Latter-day Saints, 1890–1930* (Urbana: University of Illinois Press, 1996).

57. Alexander, *Mormonism in Transition*.

Chapter Three. An Eternal Requirement

1. Joseph White Musser, Journal, March 12, 1921.

2. "John Taylor: Defender of the Faith," *Truth* 3, no. 4 (September 1937): 87.

3. "A Re-Statement of Faith," *Truth* 4, no. 1 (June 1, 1938): 5.

4. Sarah M. S. Pearsall, *Polygamy: An Early American History* (New Haven, CT: Yale University Press, 2019), 7.

5. Joseph White Musser, "Sermon, February 11, 1945," in *The Sermons of Joseph W. Musser, 1940–1945, Vols 1 and 2*, 2nd ed., edited by Nathan and Bonnie Taylor (NP: Messenger Publications, 2004–2008), 264.

6. "Reading References on Celestial Marriage," *Truth* 5, no. 2 (December 1, 1936): 2.

7. Joseph White Musser, *Celestial or Plural Marriage: The Mormon Marriage System* (Salt Lake City, 1944), 8.

8. Musser, *Celestial or Plural Marriage*, 7.

9. William Victor Smith, *Textual Studies of the Doctrine and Covenants: The Plural Marriage Revelation* (Salt Lake City: Greg Kofford, 2018), 115.

10. Smith, *Textual Studies*, 105.

11. Musser, *Celestial or Plural Marriage*, 12.

12. Smith, *Textual Studies*, 4.

13. "Bulletin No. 233," *Truth* 3, no. 1 (August 1, 1935): 26.

14. Smith, *Textual Studies*, 1.

15. Peter Coviello, *Make Yourselves Gods: Mormonism and the Unfinished Business of American Secularism* (Chicago: University of Chicago Press), 55.

16. Musser, *Celestial or Plural Marriage*, 14.

17. Musser, *Celestial or Plural Marriage*, 14.

18. Brigham Young, August 19, 1866, *Journal of Discourses* (London: LDS Booksellers, 1854–86), 11: 269.

19. "Conference Notes," *Truth* 1, no. 6 (November 1, 1935): 69.

20. Musser, *Celestial or Plural Marriage*, 14.

21. Musser, Journal, February 8, 1902.

22. Coviello, *Make Yourselves Gods*, 55.

23. Musser, *Michael, Our Father and Our God*, 10.

24. Julie Byrne, *The Other Catholics: Remaking America's Largest Religion* (New York: Columbia University Press, 2016).

25. Musser, *Celestial or Plural Marriage*.

26. "Are the Saints Ashamed of the Gospel?," *Truth* 2, no. 10 (March 1, 1937): 161.

27. Stephen C. Taysom, "A Uniform and Common Recollection: Joseph Smith's Legacy, Polygamy, and the Creation of Mormon Public Memory, 1852–2002," *Dialogue* 35, no. 3 (Fall 2002): 113–44.

28. Musser, *Celestial or Plural Marriage*, 6.

29. Musser, *Celestial or Plural Marriage*, 12.

30. Musser, *Celestial or Plural Marriage*, 12.

31. *Woolley School of the Prophets Meeting Minutes*, transcribed and edited by Bryan Buchanan, 5. Photocopies in author's possession.

32. *Woolley School of the Prophets Meeting Minutes*, 5.

33. Wilford Woodruff journal, September 25, 1890, MS 1352, Church History Library, Salt Lake City.

34. "Official Declaration," *Deseret Evening News*, September 25, 1890.

35. "Was the Manifesto a Revelation?," *Truth* 1, no. 7 (December 1935): 19.

36. "Announcement," *Truth* 1, no. 1 (June 1, 1935): 1.

37. "Announcement," *Truth* 1, no. 1 (June 1, 1935): 1.

38. According to the Church of Jesus Christ of Latter-day Saints, 7.9 percent of new marriages between 1890 and 1903 were polygamous. "The Manifesto and the End of Plural Marriage," https://www.churchofjesuschrist.org/study/manual/gospel-topics-essays/the-manifesto-and-the-end-of-plural-marriage?lang=eng.

39. "Was the Manifesto a Revelation?," 8.

40. "Was the Manifesto a Revelation?," 8.

41. "Official Statement on Plural Marriage, June 17, 1933," in *Messages of the First Presidency*, edited by James R. Clark, vol. 5 (Salt Lake City: Deseret Book, 2009).

42. "Was the Manifesto a Revelation?," 21.

43. Coviello, *Make Yourselves Gods*, 25.

44. Eliza R. Snow, "The Ultimatum of Human Life," in *Poems, Religious, Historical and Political. Also Two Articles in Prose* (Salt Lake City: Latter-day Saints Printing and Publishing, 1877): 8–9.

45. Drew Briney, ed., *Joseph W. Musser's Book of Remembrances* (n.p.: Hindsight Publications, 2010), 7.

46. Briney, *Joseph W. Musser's Book of Remembrances*, 7.

47. Briney, *Joseph W. Musser's Book of Remembrances*, 7.

48. Joseph W. Musser, "Mother's Day," *Truth* 3, no. 12 (May 1938), 210.

49. Musser, "Mother's Day," *Truth* 3, no. 12 (May 1938), 210.

50. Musser, "Mother's Day," *Truth* 3, no. 12 (May 1938), 210.

51. Musser, Journal, February 16, 1914.

52. "Bulletin No. 233," *Truth* 3, no. 1 (August 1, 1935): 26.

53. "Veiled Apologies," *Truth* 3, no. 5 (October 1, 1937): 73.

54. Pearsall, *Polygamy*, 273.

55. Joseph W. Musser, "Relief Problems," *Truth* 2, no. 1 (June 1936): 5–6.

56. Joseph White Musser, *Autobiography and Journals of Saint Joseph White Musser (1929–1949): A Brief Sketch of the Life, Labors and Faith of Saint Joseph White Musser* (n.p. n.d.), 59.

57. Letter to Joseph White Musser from Heber J. Grant, November 27, 1928. Original in private collection. Photocopy in author's possession.

58. "Veiled Apologies," 74.

59. Belinda Pratt, *Defence of Polygamy, by a Lady of Utah, in a Letter to Her Sister in New Hampshire* (1854), MS243.9 P916d 1854a, LDS Church History Library, 4.

60. Pratt, *Defence of Polygamy*, 4.

61. Rhea A. Kunz, *Polluted Fountains: An L.D.S. Look at Abortion and Other Abominations* (n.p., 1974), 46. For Hammon's account, see Lynn L. Bishop and Steven L. Bishop, *John W. Woolley, Lorin C. Woolley, the Keys of the Priesthood, the Council of Friends, and the Mormon Fundamentalists* (Latter Day Publications, 2010).

62. Cristina Rosetti, "Further Light Pertaining to Celestial Marriage: The Law of Purity and Twentieth-Century Mormon Fundamentalist Discourse on Sexuality," *Journal of Mormon History* 45, no. 3 (July 2019): 111–32.

63. Lynn L. Bishop and Steven L. Bishop, *John W. Woolley*, 205. Broadbent went on to accept the law of purity and its importance for living plural celestial marriage.

64. Bishop and Bishop, *John W. Woolley*, 205. According to Lynn L. Bishop and Steven L. Bishop's account in *John W. Woolley, Lorin C. Woolley, the Keys of the Priesthood, the Council of Friends, and the Mormon Fundamentalists*, John Y. Barlow did not have a testimony in the higher law of chastity. As a consequence, he was not allowed to take additional plural wives. Members of the "Barlow group," who did not follow Musser after his death, did not continue to teach this law.

65. Musser, "Book of Remembrance," 77.

66. Musser, *Celestial or Plural Marriage*, 8.

67. "The Short Creek Embroglio," *Truth* 1, no. 5 (October 1, 1935): 50.

68. "The Short Creek Embroglio," *Truth* 1, no. 5 (October 1, 1935): 50.

69. Marianne T. Watson, "The 1948 Secret Marriage of Louis J. Barlow," *Dialogue* 40, no. 1 (Spring 2007): 87.

Chapter Four. That the Poor May Be Exalted

1. Joseph White Musser, Journal, March 5, 1930.

2. University of Utah School of Business, "Measures of Economic Changes in Utah, 1847–1947," *Utah Economic and Business Review* 7, no. 1 (December 1947): 23.

3. Colleen McDannell, *Sister Saints: Mormon Women since the End of Polygamy* (Oxford: Oxford University Press, 2018), 57.

4. Randy Powell, "Social Welfare at the End of the World: How the Mormons Created an Alternative to the New Deal and Helped Build Modern Conservatism," *Journal of Policy History* 31, no. 4 (2019): 489.

5. "Chapter Thirty-Nine: The Church during the Great Depression," *Church History in the Fulness of Times Student Manual* (Salt Lake City: Church of Jesus Christ of Latter-day Saints, 2003), 509.

6. Powell, "Social Welfare," 490.

7. Brian Q. Cannon, "Mormons and the New Deal: The 1936 Presidential Election in Utah," *Utah Historical Quarterly* 67, no. 1 (1999): 4–22.

8. Moses 7:8.

9. See Joseph W. Musser, *The Economic Order of Heaven: Setting Forth True Communism-Socialism-Capitalism as Ordained by God for the Economic Salvation of His People* (Salt Lake City: Truth Publishing, 1948).

10. Joseph W. Musser, *Economic Order*, 1.

11. *Conference Reports of the Church of Jesus Christ of Latter-day Saints* (Salt Lake City: Deseret Book, October 1933), 5.

12. "Conference Topics," *Truth* 1, no. 12 (May 1, 1936): 168.

13. Musser, Journal, May 26, 1902.

14. Musser, Journal, September 17, 1902.

15. Musser, Journal, September 17, 1902.

16. Musser, *Economic Order*, 1.

17. Musser, *Economic Order*, 1.

18. Musser, *Economic Order*, 1.

19. Musser, *Economic Order*, 21–22.

20. "Conference Topics," *Truth* 1, no. 12 (May 1, 1936): 168–69.

21. David Walker, *Railroading Religion: Mormons, Tourists, and the Corporate Spirit of the West* (Chapel Hill: University of North Carolina Press, 2019), and Cristina Rosetti, "No Poor among Them: Poverty and Mormonism's Trek toward Secularism," *Mormon Studies Review* 9 (2023): 21–30.

22. Musser, Journal, April 8, 1935.

23. Musser, *Economic Order*, 27.

24. Musser, *Economic Order*, 8.

25. Musser, *Economic Order*, 6.

26. Doctrine and Covenants 38:27.

27. Musser, *Economic Order*, 21.

28. Joseph W. Musser, *A Priesthood Issue* (Salt Lake City: Truth Publishing, 1948), 17.

29. Musser, *A Priesthood Issue*, 17.

30. Joseph W. Musser and J. Leslie Broadbent, *Priesthood Items: Extracted from Supplement to the New and Everlasting Covenant of Marriage* (Salt Lake City: Truth Publishing, 1934), 8.

31. Musser and Broadbent, *Priesthood Items*, 11.

32. Joseph Lyman Jessop journals, July 6, 1952. Photocopy in author's possession.

33. "Economic Law of Heaven," *Truth* 4, no. 4 (September 1, 1938): 67.

34. Joseph W. Musser, "Economic Law of Heaven," *Truth* 4, no. 1 (June 1938): 9–12.

35. Musser, "Economic Law of Heaven," *Truth* 4, no. 1 (June 1938): 9–12.

36. Musser, *Economic Order*, 22.

37. Musser, *Economic Order*, 22.

38. "Economic Law of Heaven," *Truth* 4, no. 4 (September 1938): 66.

39. "Economic Law of Heaven," *Truth* 4, no. 4 (September 1938): 71.

40. Musser, *Economic Order*, 28.

41. Musser, *Economic Order*, 66–67.

42. "Economic Law of Heaven," 11.

43. "Economic Law of Heaven," 11.

44. Musser, Journal, January 31, 1942.

45. Musser, Journal, May 28, 1935.

46. Musser, Journal, June 13, 1935.

47. Musser, Journal, October 7, 1935.

48. Musser, Journal, June 19, 1935.

49. "Economic Law of Heaven," 104.

50. "God's Economic Order," *Truth* 4, no. 7 (December 1, 1938): 135.

51. Musser, Journal, June 13, 1935.

52. Musser, Journal, May 10, 1935.

53. Musser, Journal, May 10, 1935.

54. *Woolley School of the Prophets Meeting Minutes*, transcribed and edited by Bryan Buchanan, 3. Photocopies in author's possession.

55. *Woolley School of the Prophets Meeting Minutes*, 5.

Bibliographic Essay

1. Joseph White Musser, *Autobiography and Journals of Saint Joseph White Musser (1929–1949): A Brief Sketch of the Life, Labors and Faith of Saint Joseph White Musser* (n.p., n.d., January 1950), 113.

2. Joseph White Musser, Journal, August 8, 1933, in Joseph White Musser journals, 1920–1944, MS 2899, LDS Church History Library. Photocopy in author's possession.

3. Musser, Journal, April 25, 1933.

4. Musser, Journal, March 1943.

5. Musser, Joseph W. The New and Everlasting Covenant of Marriage (Salt Lake City: Truth Publishing, 1933).

Index

CRISTINA M. ROSETTI is an assistant professor
of humanities at Utah Tech University.

The University of Illinois Press
is a founding member of the
Association of University Presses.

———————————————

Composed in 10.75/14 Adobe Minion Pro
with DIN display
by Kirsten Dennison
at the University of Illinois Press
Manufactured by Sheridan Books, Inc.

University of Illinois Press
1325 South Oak Street
Champaign, IL 61820-6903
www.press.uillinois.edu